THE
REFORMATION

Martyn Whittock

Heinemann Library,
an imprint of Heinemann Publishers (Oxford) Ltd,
Halley Court, Jordan Hill, Oxford OX2 8EJ

OXFORD LONDON EDINBURGH MADRID
ATHENS BOLOGNA PARIS MELBOURNE
SYDNEY AUCKLAND SINGAPORE TOKYO
IBADAN NAIROBI HARARE GABORONE
PORTSMOUTH NH (USA)

This edition first published 1994

98 97 96 95 94

10 9 8 7 6 5 4 3 2 1

**British Library Cataloguing in Publication Data is available
on request from the British Library.**

ISBN 0–431–07353–8

Designed by Ron Kamen, Green Door Design Ltd, Basingstoke

Illustrated by Phil Burrows and Jeff Edwards

Printed in China

The front cover shows *The St Bartholomew's Day Massacre* by
François Dubois de'Amiens, an eyewitness to the event.

Acknowledgements

The author and publisher would like to thank the following for
permission to reproduce photographs:

Ancient Art & Architecture Collection: 6.5D
Archiv für Kunst und Geschichte, Berlin: 3.2D, 3.2G
Bridgeman Art Library: 2.2B (Louvre); 3.1A (Church of St
Marie, Wittenberg)
British Library: 7.1E
Bulloz: 6.2A
Mary Evans Picture Library: 2.3A
Gemäldegalerie, Staatliche Museen Preussischer Kulturbesitz,
Berlin: 7.5A
Photographie Giraudon: 3.6A (Jurgens); 5.2E
Musée Cantonal des Beaux-Arts de Lausanne: cover, 7.3A
Museum of Fine Arts, Boston: 2.4A
Roger-Viollet: 4.2D
Scala: 1.2D, 2.5D, 6.1A, 6.3B (Santa Maria Della Vittoria,
Rome)
Thuringisches Hauptstaatsarchiv Weimar: 3.3A

Every effort has been made to contact copyright holders of
material published in this book. Any omissions will be rectified
in subsequent printings if notice is given to the publisher.

Thanks also to Michael Mullet of the Department of History,
Lancaster University, for his invaluable comments on the
original manuscript.

Details of written sources

In some sources the wording or sentence structure has been
simplified to ensure that the source is accessible.

E. Cairns, *Christianity Through the Centuries*, Zondervan, 1981:
1.1B, 7.4C
E. Cameron, *The European Reformation*, OUP, 1991: 6.3A,
6.5B
M. Carter, C. Culpin, N. Kinloch, *Past into Present*, Collins,
1989: 7.1D
O. Chadwick, *The Reformation*, Penguin, 1972: 2.1A, 2.5B,
3.2A, 3.3C, 4.3D, 5.1D, 5.2B, 5.2D, 5.3B, 5.3D, 7.2A, 7.2E
N. Cohn, *The Pursuit of the Millenium*, Paladin, 1970: 4.1A,
4.2A, 4.2B
Collins Shorter Contemporary Dictionary, Collins, 1972: 2.2D
J. Davis, *Pursuit of Power*, Harper, 1970: 7.4D
J. Elliott, *Europe Divided*, Fontana, 1968: 7.3E
G. Elton, *Reformation Europe*, Collins, 1963: 3.4A, 5.2C
H. A. L. Fisher, *A History of Europe*, Collins, 1935: 1.1D, 3.3B,
7.1B, 7.3B
V. Green, *Renaissance and Reformation*, Edward Arnold, 1964:
2.1B, 7.1C
W. Hubatsch, *Government in Reformation Europe*, 1971: 3.5B
V. Kiernan, *Crisis in Europe*, Routledge, 1965: 5.1B
J. Kittelson, *Luther and the Reformation*, NP, 1989: 5.1C
R. D. Linder, *The History of Christianity*, Lion, 1990: 1.2B,
1.2C, 2.3B, 2.5C, 3.1C, 3.1E, 3.2B, 4.3B, 6.1B, 6.1C, 6.3C,
6.4D, 6.5A
R. Lockyer, *Henry VII*, Longman, 1968: 2.1C
Niccolò Machiavelli, *Mandragola*, 1517 (this edition published
by Greenwood Press): 1.1C
W. H. McNeill, *A World History*, OUP, 1979: 2.2A
A. Maczak, *Politics and Society in Reformation Europe*,
1987: 3.4D
National Geographic, October, 1983, 164(4): 1.1A, 3.1B, 3.2E,
3.2F, 3.2H, 6.2B, 6.4A, 6.5C, 7.4A, 7.5B, 7.5C
Oxford Dictionary of Quotations, OUP, 1979: 3.2C
The Penguin English Dictionary, Penguin, 1972: 2.2C
J. M. Roberts, *History of the World*, Hutchinson, 1980: 2.3C,
3.4B
W. Shirer, *The Rise and Fall of the Third Reich*, Pan Books,
1964: 3.5D
C. Strong, *The Early Modern World*, University of London,
1968: 7.3D
W. Woodruff, *The Struggle for World Power*, MacMillan, 1981:
7.4B

CONTENTS

1.1 *E*urope in 1517

In the early 16th century, the countries of Europe were not organized in the same way as they are today. For example Germany, which today is one country, was divided up into many little states. Some were ruled by princes, some by dukes, and others were ruled by men who were also bishops and archbishops in the Christian Church. The states were part of what was called the **Holy Roman Empire**. This was not really Roman. It was called this because it was supposed to be the successor of the ancient Roman Empire. The ruler of the Holy Roman Empire in 1517 was **Emperor Charles**, who was King of Spain and who also ruled land in Italy and in what is now the Netherlands and Belgium.

Italy was divided into a number of states. The **Pope**, who was the head of the Roman Catholic Church, ruled land in Italy, just like a prince or a king. These lands were called the **Papal States**. The King of France and Emperor Charles each wanted to rule parts of Italy. There were many wars between them.

In Britain, England and Scotland were separate countries with their own kings. In the east of Europe, **Poland** was much larger than it is today and the Grand Duke of Moscow had succeeded in making his city the centre of a **Russian Empire** which was growing more and more powerful.

People from Europe were beginning to discover more about the world in which they lived. In 1488 the Portuguese explorer, **Bartholomew Diaz**, sailed round the Cape of Good Hope into the Indian Ocean. In 1492 the explorer **Christopher Columbus** sailed from Spain to America. Another Portuguese, **Vasco da Gama**, sailed to India in 1498. Ships belonging to **John Cabot** sailed from Bristol to Newfoundland, in North America, in 1497. Other expeditions went from Spain to South America and from Portugal to East Africa. The European view of the world was changing. The world was much bigger and much more complicated than they had ever imagined. As explorers travelled to different countries, they met many people with different ways of life, ideas and beliefs.

In Europe there was great rivalry between the Christian countries and the **Ottoman Empire**. The Ottoman Empire was based in Turkey, but was conquering countries in Eastern Europe. It was an Islamic empire, but the conquered peoples could continue as Christians if they wished.

A Luther's Germany was not two Germanies, as today, but hundreds; a crazy quilt of territories under the Holy Roman Emperor. The seven most powerful states elected the Emperor.

M. Severy, 'National Geographic', 1983, writing about Germany in the early 16th century.

B The geographical knowledge of medieval people underwent remarkable changes between 1492 and 1600.

From 'Christianity Through the Centuries' by E. Cairns, 1981.

C Do you think that the Turks will invade Italy this year?

A woman character to her priest, in the play 'Mandragola', written by the Italian writer Machiavelli in 1517.

D But for the French and Spanish armies, Italy would have been conquered by the Turks.

From 'A History of Europe' by H. A. L. Fisher, 1935.

Under the rule of **Sultan Muhammad II**, Ottoman armies captured the Christian city of Constantinople (modern Istanbul, Turkey) from the Christians in 1453. The Ottomans raided southern Italy and were a constant threat to the Christian west. There were often wars between the Holy Roman Empire and the Ottomans.

Despite this, not all Christian countries opposed the Ottomans. Sometimes the rulers of Venice and France preferred to be friends with the Ottomans and fight the other Christian kings in Europe. We should not think that all Christian rulers were on one side and all Islamic rulers were on the other. The situation in Europe was much more complicated than this in the early 16th century. Many Christian kings were bitter rivals.

Columbus

Christopher Columbus (1451–1506) was born in Italy. This Genoese explorer was the first reliable discoverer of the American continent. His four voyages to the 'New World' were paid for by the Spanish government. His three ships – the *Santa Maria*, *Nina* and *Pinta* – sighted land in the Caribbean on October 12, 1492.

His discovery was part of a series of European 'voyages of discovery' which explored areas of the world previously unknown to Europeans. Columbus died at Valladolid, in Spain, in 1506.

—— Boundary of the Holy Roman Empire

▇ Land ruled personally by the Emperor

0   100   200   300 miles
0   200   400 km

The main countries of Europe and the Holy Roman Empire ruled by the Emperor Charles from 1519.

1.2 Christendom

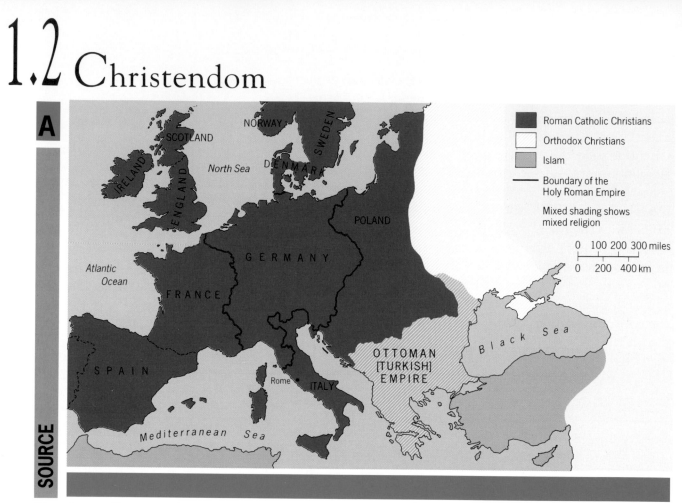

A

Roman Catholic Christians

Orthodox Christians

Islam

Boundary of the Holy Roman Empire

Mixed shading shows mixed religion

The religions of Europe in 1500.

At the beginning of the 16th century, the majority of people in Europe were Christians. Those who lived in west and central Europe belonged to the **Roman Catholic Church**. The head of this Church was the **Pope** who lived in Rome. At times there were splits in the Roman Catholic Church – there were two rival popes in 1400 and three in 1409. By the 16th century, however, these splits seemed to have stopped. In what is now Greece and Russia, Christians were members of the **Orthodox Church**. Those who lived in Greece and south-east Europe were ruled by the Turks. The Christian countries were often said to be part of **Christendom**.

The Pope was a powerful ruler as well as a Church leader. He was often involved in politics. Pope Julius II led his army into battle at the siege of the city of Mirandola, north Italy, in 1511 The English Archbishop of York also commanded an army in this war. In 1527 the Christian king Charles V of Spain actually held the Pope as his prisoner. Most popes were Italian. In the 15th century, there were only two popes who were not. Between 1523 and 1978, all the popes were Italian.

B

The nearer you get to Rome the more corruption you will find.

The Italian writer, Machiavelli (1469–1527).

C

Missionary activities in the Middle and Far East, among the Mongols and the Chinese, declined and died out after the middle of the 14th century.

From 'The History of Christianity' by R. D. Linder, 1990.

Most people sincerely believed in God, even if they disapproved of some of the things done by leaders of the Church. During the 15th century, many people paid priests to pray for them after they died. These priests were called **chantry priests**. Pictures and statues of Jesus on the cross became very popular in churches. People were showing that they wanted to feel closer to God; they wanted to be sure that He loved them. When people criticized the Church, it was not because they did not believe any more, it was because they wanted the Church to be better.

A 16th-century painting by the artist Mathis Grünewald, showing the suffering of Jesus on the cross.

D

SOURCE

Machiavelli

Niccoló Machiavelli (1469–1527) was born in Florence. As a political writer and diplomat he believed that rulers should use a combination of intelligence, cunning and brutality in order to stay in power. His ideas were encouraged by the belief that only such a ruler could survive in the dangerous conditions in Italy during his lifetime. He praised the Borgia family's ruthless rule in Florence. He travelled to Switzerland, Germany and France on behalf of the rulers of Florence. When the Medici family came to power in Florence he was briefly imprisoned; later he wrote the book *The Prince* about how a ruler should keep political power.

E

SOURCE

The scandal starts in Rome and runs through the whole clergy. They are worse than Turks. They do anything for gold. They only ring their bells for coins and only attend vespers [a church service] when they get something out of it.

Savonarola (1452–98), an Italian monk who was famous for his sermons against the Pope.

2.1 Rulers against the Pope

Although the kings and queens of western Europe were Christians, they sometimes had serious arguments with the Pope. The Church owned land in many countries. The Pope's power was not as great as it had once been, but some rulers disliked the fact that the Pope still seemed rich and powerful. They also felt that they should have the final say in the running of their countries. They resented it when popes tried to interfere. This feeling was often shared by the merchants in the growing towns. Some of them wanted to be free of the control of the Church. Often they had to pay taxes to the Church, which they did not like. Some cities in Germany were actually ruled by bishops of the Church and **clergy** (priests) paid no taxes. This was unpopular.

In a number of countries, powerful kings and queens began to act more freely. This was not new, but during the 15th century it became more common. In England, **King Henry VII** (reigned 1485–1509) was determined to be a strong king. This was continued by his son, **Henry VIII**. In Spain, the same was true of **King Ferdinand** and **Queen Isabella**. The Holy Roman Emperor Charles V was also prepared to go against the Pope if he disagreed with him.

In all these countries the rulers were making the running of the country more organized. They were improving the ways in which taxes were collected and the law courts were run. The people in some of these countries began to feel a real pride in their country. This is called **patriotism**. They began to think of the Pope as a foreigner who interfered in their country. This could be seen in England, Scotland, the Netherlands and in some of the cities of Switzerland and Germany.

The Pope kept more power in countries which were divided, or which were less well run by a weaker monarch. However, even in Scotland where the power of the monarch was weaker, the Church was becoming less powerful.

Since the Pope could not rely on rulers agreeing with him, he had to discuss what he wanted, or **negotiate**, with them. He began to send ambassadors, called **nuncios**, to the courts of the rulers of Europe. The first nuncio was sent to Venice in 1500. Another nuncio was sent to Paris in 1513.

A **SOURCE**

The Pope was becoming weaker because governments were becoming stronger. And the stronger the government, the more helpless lay the vast wealth of the Church.

From 'The Reformation' by O. Chadwick, 1972.

B **SOURCE**

Until the election of a pro-Spanish pope in 1591, his relations with successive popes were bad. He was determined to be the absolute master of the Church. Time and again Philip placed the interests of Spain before those of the Roman Catholic Church.

The actions of Philip II, King of Spain. From 'Renaissance and Reformation' by V. Green, 1964.

C **SOURCE**

Henry was limited by what had been done in the past and by law. Spiritual and moral matters fell within the authority of the Church. These were boundaries which Henry recognized.

The King of England. From 'Henry VII' by R. Lockyer, 1968.

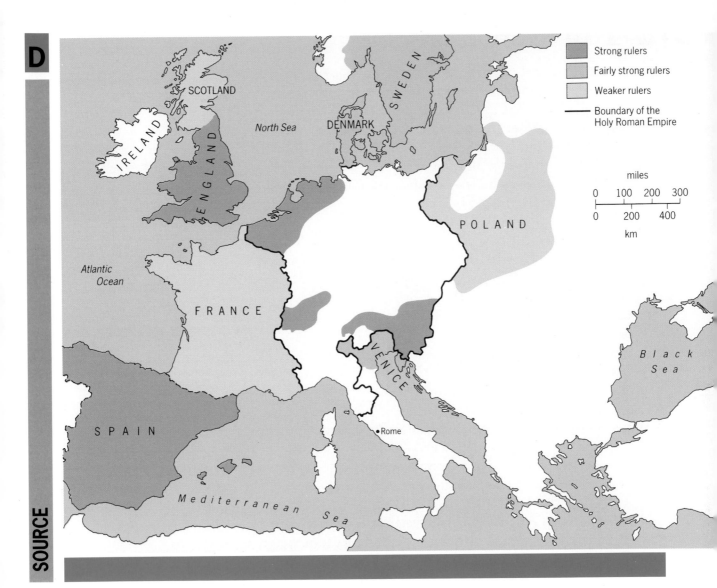

The power of the European rulers in the early 16th century.

The King of France has the power to:
- appoint 10 archbishops
- appoint 82 bishops
- appoint 527 abbots.

Rights of the King of France agreed with the Pope by the Concordat of Bologna, in 1516.

Henry VII

King Henry VII (1457–1509) was born during the English Wars of the Roses between the two rival royal families of York and Lancaster. Because of this he had a weak claim to the English throne. He was forced into exile by the Yorkist King Edward IV. Despite this, he led a rebellion against King Richard III, and defeated and killed him at the battle of Bosworth, 1485. Henry was determined to put an end to the wars which had divided England in the 15th century and to keep power in the hands of his family, the Tudors. By marrying Elizabeth of York he united the two rival royal families. He put down all attempts to threaten his rule, kept England out of foreign wars and made the government more efficient and prosperous. Under the Tudors, English kings became more powerful than before.

2.2 The Renaissance

During the 19th century, historians studied the changes which had taken place in Europe from the 14th to the 16th centuries. They realized that many ideas changed in this particular period of history. One of these changes was that people began to think more about the ideas and ways of life which had been popular with the **Greeks** and **Romans** centuries before. To these 19th-century historians it seemed as if ideas which had been dead for centuries were reborn at this time. As a result, they called this period of history the **Renaissance**. This word means 'rebirth'. Historians still use this word when looking at this period of history, even though they realize that the changes which were happening were very complicated. In fact, many of the old ways of doing things carried on despite the Renaissance.

The interest in ancient Greek and Roman ideas began in Italy. With new enthusiasm, educated people began to search for and study books written centuries before. These people became known as **Humanists**. Some Humanists were important members of the Church. One of these was **Pope Martin V** who became Pope in 1417. Other Humanists were against the way the rulers of the Church tried to control what people studied. They wanted to study and make up their own minds.

In 1480 the Italian **Angelo Poliziano** became Professor of the study of Greek in Florence. This was important because the New Testament was written in Greek by the first Christians. As more people began to study Greek they were able to discover for themselves the message of the Bible. This challenged the authority and power of the Roman Catholic Church. The Church believed that it alone should decide what was right or wrong, even if it differed from what the Bible said. Humanists began to say that people should live in the way written in the Bible, not in the way that the rulers of the Church said.

The ideas of the Renaissance spread to other parts of Europe. A man named **Erasmus** (1469–1536) from Rotterdam (in the modern Netherlands) became a famous scholar. He attacked church leaders who behaved badly and made fun of those people who opposed the new way of studying. In his books ***The Christian Soldier's Manual*** and ***The Colloquies*** he wrote about the way people should behave, in order to please God.

Some of the important cities in Italy during the Renaissance.

A

SOURCE

The Renaissance had, of course, taken place in Italy from about 1350. With its memories of Roman greatness, it naturally had strong appeal to Italians.

From 'A World History' by W. H. McNeill, 1979.

B

SOURCE

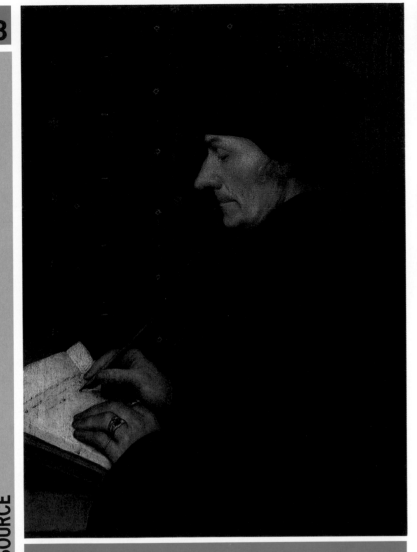

Erasmus of Rotterdam, painted by Hans Holbein the Younger, 1523.

C

SOURCE

The **Renaissance**: the revival of interest in ancient Greek art and learning in the 15th and 16th centuries.

'The Penguin English Dictionary', 1969.

D

SOURCE

Renaissance: great revival of learning in the 14th to 16th centuries.

'Collins Shorter Contemporary Dictionary', 1972.

Erasmus

Desiderius Erasmus (1469–1536) was born in the Netherlands, and was one the most important thinkers and writers in Europe. He was educated by a group called the **devotio moderna** who believed in the importance of education and in helping the poor as part of a Christian's duty to God. He studied and joined the **Augustinian** religious group within the Catholic Church. While he was in Paris he became convinced that the Humanists were right in their way of studying and thinking.

He visited England and lectured at the universities of Oxford and Cambridge. He became friends with English thinkers such as Thomas More and John Fisher, who encouraged him to study the Bible. He looked at the New Testament in the original Greek language and travelled in Italy, meeting other Humanist thinkers. This helped Erasmus to challenge the claim of the rulers of the Church that they were the only people who could decide on the meaning of the Bible.

2.3 Printing

Today we take books for granted. They are produced on machines in their millions. However, before the middle of the 15th century, books were written by hand. This slowed down the spread of ideas. Handwritten books were expensive and few people ever owned one. For most people it was not worth learning to read.

The first people to experiment with printing lived in Asia. In the 5th century, the **Chinese** began to print words and pictures using wooden blocks. The first known printed book was Chinese and it dates from about 868.

Although printing was a very important invention, it does not seem to have spread to Europe. When Europeans experimented with printing in the 15th century they thought that they were doing it for the very first time.

A printing shop, around 1500.

A

SOURCE

In 1445 **Johann Gutenberg** began to print words using **movable metal type**. Letters were cut in metal and fitted together to make words. They were then inked and pressed down on to paper. The very first printed book in Europe was the 'Gutenberg' Bible (1456).

The invention of printing was helped by a number of other inventions. From the 12th century, Italian cloth workers began to experiment with printing patterns on cloth. From the mid-14th century, better quality paper was being made from mashed-up rags. This paper was made for writing but it was eventually used for printing. Neither of these two ways of doing things were deliberately done to make printing happen. But, they smoothed the way for the spread of printing. After Gutenberg began printing in Mainz, Germany, the skill of printing began to spread. There were printing presses in Rome in 1467, Paris in 1470, Cracow (Poland) in 1474, London in 1476.

The new invention led to a huge number of books being produced. These early editions of books are called **incunabula**. By 1550 there were between 15 and 20 million copies of individual books in Europe. The ideas in these books were being spread in a way that had never been known before. When a printer in Paris heard that one of Erasmus' books was about to be banned by the University of the Sorbonne, he quickly printed 24,000 copies. Books were no longer rare. Many people wanted to read them. They wanted to read the ideas for themselves.

Caxton

William Caxton (1422–91) was born in Kent. Caxton was the first English printer. Before his work, all books produced in England had been written by hand. He lived for some time in Bruges, modern Belgium, where he became an important leader of the English merchants living in Flanders and Holland. In 1470 he became financial adviser to the Duchess of Burgundy.

While living in Bruges, and then in Cologne in Germany, he began to translate books into English. In 1475 he printed the first book in English, which was a history of the Trojan wars of ancient Greece. In 1476 he returned to England to set up a printing press there.

Caxton's printed books were not particularly beautiful books, but they were much cheaper to buy than handwritten books. He had printed 100 titles by the time he died in 1491.

B

SOURCE

I wish that the Scriptures might be translated into all languages so that not only the Scots and the Irish but also the Turks might read and understand them. I long that the farm labourer might sing them as he follows the plough.

From the writings of Erasmus (1469–1536).

C

The culture which resulted from the coming of printing was as different from any earlier one as it is from one which takes radio and television for granted. The modern age is the age of print.

From 'History of the World' by J. M. Roberts, 1980.

2.4 New Ideas in the Church

In the 16th century, many people came together to criticize the way that the Church was run. This was not new. For many years, men and women within the Roman Catholic Church had found things about it that they did not agree with.

Some of the people who suggested reforms wanted the Church to be totally changed. They sometimes claimed that leaders of the Church were not true Christians because they were not living the way God wanted them to. This claim was very unpopular with the powerful people in the Church. The leaders of the Church would often accuse their critics of being **heretics**. This meant that they were not real Christians and could be punished for what they said and believed.

In Europe in the 14th century there had been a great disagreement between monks belonging to the Order of St Francis. Some of these monks said that it was wrong for the Church to be so rich and powerful. They claimed that real Christians should live simple lives and not aim to own large amounts of property. These monks were called **Spiritual Franciscans**. In England in the late 14th and 15th centuries there was a group of people known as the **Lollards**. They were followers of **John Wyclif**, who died in 1384. The Lollards read Wyclif's English **translation** of the Latin Bible and used it to condemn the rich and powerful Roman Catholic Church.

In Germany, **John of Wessel** (1400–81) claimed that it was the Bible which should tell people what was right and wrong, not the leaders of the Church. He was arrested and sentenced to life imprisonment in a monastery at Mainz.

A SOURCE

'Knight, Death, and the Devil' by Albrecht Dürer (1471–1528). It shows that a Christian is like an armed knight fighting all that is bad in the world.

B SOURCE

It is Jesus who you must love and keep to be your friend. When all else fades away he will not leave you. Whether you want to or not, one day you must leave everything behind. So keep close to Jesus in life as well as in death for only he can help you when everything else fails.

From 'The Imitation of Christ' by Thomas à Kempis (1380–1471).

Some changes in the way that people of the 15th century showed their love for God.

People came to think more about the suffering of Jesus.

More people used rosary beads to help them count and remember their prayers.

People prayed more often to the Virgin Mary.

At Easter, people had processions around their churches. It reminded them of how Jesus carried his cross and was crucified.

Not all Roman Catholics were so revolutionary. Some wanted to change the Church more gradually. These people included members of a movement called the **devotio moderna** (the modern way of serving God). For them it was important to live a holy life, to help the poor and sick and to improve education. One of the early members of this movement was **Geert Groote**, who died in 1384. He formed a community of people who lived in Deventer in the Netherlands. They called themselves the **Brethren of the Common Life**. During the 15th century, they set up communities in Germany and Switzerland.

Thomas à Kempis (1380–1471) was educated by these people. He wrote a very popular book, ***The Imitation of Christ***, which encouraged people to have faith in Jesus and to live a life of love as Jesus had done. Many Roman Catholics wanted to try to live 'Christ-like' lives.

Thomas à Kempis

Originally known as Thomas Hemerken (1380–1471), he was born in Kempten, in Germany. In about 1392 he went to live in Deventer, in the Netherlands. Here there was a religious community devoted to education and care for the poor. Later he moved to the monastery at Agnietenberg where he lived for the next 70 years until his death.

At the Agnietenberg monastery he copied handwritten books and trained young monks. His most famous book, *Imitation of Christ*, is well known for its simple and easily understood language. In it Thomas explained how the most fulfilled and happy life would come from obeying Jesus, and not being obsessed with possessions.

2.5 Reasons for Change

From 1517 there were tremendous changes in the Roman Catholic Church in Europe. Since almost everyone was a member of the Church, this had a great impact on the lives of ordinary people. Also, because the Church was so powerful politically, the reforms changed the way in which many countries were run. Historians call these great changes the **Reformation**. The changes were so important that the Reformation is sometimes called a **turning point** in the history of Europe. This means that the way in which many people thought and acted changed because of it.

When looking at such an important series of events, historians often ask questions like 'why did this happen when it did?'. They are looking for the **causes** of something happening. Historians divide the reasons why something happened into **long-term** causes and **short-term** causes. Long-term causes are those which have been building up for a long time. Short-term causes are things which happen shortly before an event. Often, people are more aware of the short-term causes because they happen just before a big event or action. However, the long-term causes are just as important.

For a long time, many people had been unhappy with the way in which the Church was run. Some felt that the Pope was too rich and powerful. They felt that he did not rule the Church like a man of God but just like any other rich prince. **Rodrigo Borgia** had even bribed people into making him Pope. As Pope Alexander VI (1492–1503), he did what he could to make his own family rich. This was doubly shocking – priests were not allowed to marry or have sexual partners.

Some priests and monks did not live holy lives. We have seen how men and women began to criticize the Church. Educated people wanted to make up their own minds about the Bible. The ideas of the Renaissance, spread by printing, made them question the right of the Church to tell them how to live their lives.

Since the 13th century, merchants and shopkeepers in towns had become more important. They wanted to make a profit from trade. They resented the way in which the Church controlled people's lives. Some of their views were shared by kings and queens who wanted to reduce the power and wealth of the Church in their countries.

A **SOURCE**

Now that we have got to be Pope, let us enjoy it.

Pope Leo X, when he became Pope in 1513.

B **SOURCE**

A priest known to be guilty of murder was seen to escape with a light imprisonment. A parish priest kept a woman and was not punished. Too many scandals, too many injustices, too much inefficiency.

From 'The Reformation' by O. Chadwick, 1972.

C **SOURCE**

Now no one disagrees with anything that happens. No one opposes anything.

A speaker at the 5th Lateran Council (1517), talking about how nearly everyone at the council agreed that things were all right in the Church.

In the early years of the 16th century, the situation became more tense. Between 1512 and 1517 there were several great meetings of the important people of the Church. This was called the **5th Lateran Council**. It did very little to improve the way the Church was run, however. Pope Leo X, who became Pope in 1513, showed no interest in living a holy life.

The Pope tried to increase the money that German Christians paid to the Church. This was very unpopular in parts of Germany such as **Saxony** where the **cost of living** was already becoming expensive. Despite the fact that many Germans resented giving large amounts of money to the Church it was difficult for them to make a stand against the Pope. Germany was not a united country.

Lucrezia Borgia

Lucrezia Borgia (1480–1519) was the daughter of the Spanish cardinal Rodrigo Borgia, who bribed his way to become Pope Alexander VI, and his mistress Vannozza Catanei. Lucrezia was married three times as part of her father's and brother's political plans.

Her first husband was Giovanni Sforza, lord of Pesaro, in Italy. Later he fell out with her father and fled for his life, claiming that Lucrezia was having an affair with her own father, who was now the Pope.

Her father then had her marry a member of the ruling family of Naples. In 1500 this man was wounded by assassins. While recovering he was strangled on the orders of Lucrezia's brother, Cesare Borgia.

Shortly afterwards Lucrezia had a son who was accused of being either her brother's child, or more probably her father's.

In 1501 she married Alfonso from the ruling family of Ferrara, Italy. When her father died in 1503 she stopped being active in politics.

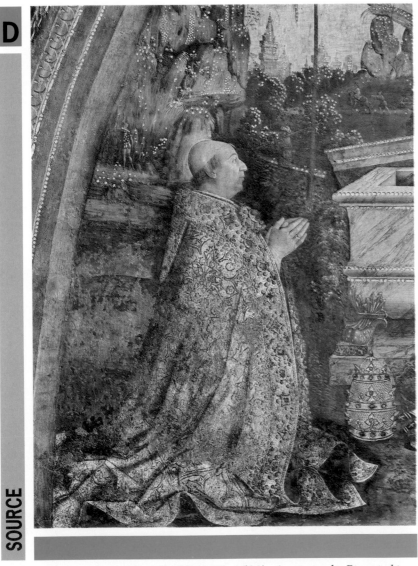

Rodrigo Borgia as Pope Alexander VI (1492–1503). A painting by Pinturicchio.

3.1 Martin Luther

In the Middle Ages most Roman Catholics believed that when Christians died they did not go to heaven straight away. Instead their souls went to a place called **purgatory**. In purgatory they were punished for the wrong things that they had done in their lives. When they had been punished enough, they would then go to heaven. People who had lived very bad lives and who were not sorry went to hell. Only the very good went straight to heaven.

Many Roman Catholics believed that it was possible to help a friend or a relative who had died and who was in purgatory. They believed that prayer or a **pilgrimage** to a holy place would help the souls in purgatory. Roman Catholics would also buy **indulgences**. The Church promised that the money they paid would shorten the time that the soul of a dead friend or loved-one had to spend in purgatory.

In 1514 a German nobleman, Albert, became the Archbishop of Mainz, Germany. He paid the Pope a lot of money to get this position. The Pope needed a lot of money in order to build the new church of St Peter in Rome. Albert had borrowed the money he paid the Pope. To get some of it back he arranged to have indulgences sold in his lands. Some of the money he was paid would go to those who had given him loans and some would go to the Pope. The man put in charge of selling these indulgences was a Dominican monk named **Johann Tetzel**.

Martin Luther was a monk at the **University of Wittenberg**. He was the Professor of Biblical Studies. He thought that it was wrong to sell indulgences. He knew that there was no mention of it in the Bible. He also believed that people went to heaven by having faith in God. It was not possible to **buy** forgiveness of wrong doings.

On October 31, 1517 he nailed an essay to the door of the Castle church. In it he gave 95 reasons why he disagreed with Church practice. They are known as the **95 Theses**. His complaints were not revolutionary. They were quite moderate. However, many people were glad to see them. For a long time people in Germany had grown tired of the way the Church was run. The 95 Theses were copied without Luther's permission and they spread across Germany in a few weeks.

A
SOURCE

A *painting of Luther in the pulpit by Cranach the Elder (1472–1553), one of Luther's friends.*

B
SOURCE

Martin is a brilliant man. The whole row is due to the jealousy of the monks. It is only a monks' quarrel.

Pope Leo X, in 1518, talking about Martin Luther.

C
SOURCE

Today most Roman Catholics and Protestants would say that several generations before Luther's protest against indulgences, there was something radically wrong with the Roman Catholic Church.

From 'The History of Christianity' by R. Linder, 1990.

A 16th-century cartoon about the Roman Catholic Church.

One piece of Jesus' baby clothes, one piece of the burning bush, one piece of bread from the Last Supper, five drops of milk from the Virgin Mary.

A list of the so-called 'Holy Relics' that could be seen in the Castle church, Wittenberg, in 1509. It was believed that a visit to this church could save a pilgrim from 1,902,202 years in purgatory.

Luther sent a copy of his protest to Archbishop Albert. Albert was very angry. He decided to 'crush the rash monk of Wittenberg'. He complained to the Pope that Luther was challenging the power of the rulers of the Church. Luther heard how angry the archbishop was, but he refused to **recant**. This means that he would not take back what he had said.

Albert was not the only one against Luther. Johann Tetzel, who sold the indulgences, belonged to a group of monks called **Dominicans**. Luther belonged to a group called the **Augustinians**. There was bad feeling between the two groups of monks and the Dominicans' leader, **Cardinal Cajetan**, joined the attack on Luther.

In 1519 Luther was asked to go to Leipzig to explain himself. Here he met great opposition in an important debate. Faced with these attacks he criticized other things he believed were wrong with the Church. His enemies were pushing him into a corner. He responded by making more criticisms. In 1520 he published a book, ***The Babylonian Captivity of the Church***. In it he accused the Pope of betraying the Christian faith.

Pope Leo X

Originally named Giovanni de' Medici (1475–1521) he was born in Florence, Italy, into the ruling family of Florence. Educated in Florence and at the University of Pisa, he became Pope in 1513.

Leo spent huge amounts of money on church buildings in Rome, books for the Vatican Library and works of art. He did little to reform the Catholic Church. It was Leo who rejected Luther's call for reform and excommunicated him in 1521.

3.2 Rebellion

At first Martin Luther had only moderate criticisms of the Church. By 1520 the opposition he faced had turned him into a revolutionary. The Pope sent him a message saying that Luther was in the wrong and demanding that he recant. This type of document is known as a **bull**. Luther took the bull and burnt it by the Old Elster Gate at Wittenberg.

On January 3, 1521 the Pope **excommunicated** Luther. This meant that Luther was thrown out of the Church and that the Pope and other Roman Catholics thought he would go to hell when he died. Nobody should have anything to do with him. In Rome a model of Luther was burned at the stake. This was what his enemies wanted to do to him.

Luther lived in the part of Germany known as **Saxony**. Saxony was ruled by the Elector Frederick. However, Saxony was also part of the Holy Roman Empire. The ruler of the Empire and the lord of Elector Frederick was the Emperor Charles V.

Frederick was an important man. Both the Emperor and the Pope were keen to keep him as a friend. Neither of them wanted to upset him. This helped Luther because Frederick was determined to protect him as one of his subjects. Frederick would not hand Luther over to his enemies. Neither the Pope nor the Emperor could arrest him themselves because this would have annoyed Frederick.

In April, 1521 Luther was ordered to go to a meeting of the leaders of the Holy Roman Empire. The meeting was known as a **Diet**. The Diet that Luther was called to was in the city of **Worms**, Germany. It is known as the **Diet of Worms**. At the Diet, Luther still refused to take back what he had said and written. After he had left the Diet, the members issued an order that Luther was to be arrested and his books burned. No one had arrested him at the Diet because he had **safe conduct** to go there.

A To go against the conscience is neither safe nor right. God help me. Amen.

Luther speaking at the Diet of Worms, 1521, quoted in 'The Reformation' by O. Chadwick, 1972.

B To go against the conscience is neither safe nor open to us. On this I take my stand. I can do no other. God help me. Amen.

Luther speaking at the Diet of Worms, 1521, quoted in 'The History of Christianity', 1990.

C Here I stand. I can do no other. God help me. Amen.

Luther speaking at the Diet of Worms, 1521, quoted in 'Oxford Dictionary of Quotations', 1979.

A painting by Anton von Werner (1843–1915) of the 'The Diet of Worms', 1521.

I am descended from a long line of Christian emperors. A single monk who goes against all Christianity for a thousand years must be wrong.

Emperor Charles V commenting on Martin Luther at the Diet of Worms, 1521.

Farewell unhappy, hopeless blasphemous Rome! The wrath of God has come upon you as you deserved.

Luther speaking as he burned the bull, 1520.

On the way home from the Diet, Luther was seized by Frederick's soldiers. To protect him from his enemies he was taken to **Wartburg Castle**. No one in Wittenberg knew that he was there. He was given the name 'squire George' to keep his real identity a secret. While he was in hiding he translated the New Testament from Greek into German.

Frederick III

Frederick III (1463–1525) was born in Torgau, modern Germany. He was known as Frederick the Wise. He was ruler, or **Elector**, of Saxony from 1486. Helped by the Archbishop of Henneberg, he tried to reform the Holy Roman Empire by reducing the power of its ruler, the Emperor. He refused to become Emperor himself but in 1519 supported the election of the Emperor Charles V.

Frederick appointed Luther and his friend Melanchthon to work in the University of Wittenberg. He refused to ban, or arrest, Luther after he was condemned by the Pope. He collected religious relics and encouraged artists such as Albrecht Dürer and Lucas Cranach the Elder. He died without an heir because he had never married.

Martin Luther probably never met the Elector Frederick. Frederick thought that Luther was too revolutionary, but still protected him. Without this protection Luther would probably have been arrested and burned.

While Luther was in Wartburg Castle his friend **Philip Melanchthon** continued to spread Luther's ideas. Both he and Luther wanted the Church to change gradually. They had never intended to break away from the Roman Catholic Church. They still hoped that the Pope would agree with their opinions in time. Melanchthon believed in this even more than Luther.

Other people wanted the Church to change much faster. They were not patient. One of these was **Andreas Karlstadt**. He encouraged the people in Wittenberg to smash the statues in the churches. He accused the people of being **superstitious**. **Nicholas Storch** and **Markus Stübner** also wanted radical change. They were called the **Zwickau Prophets**.

G

SOURCE

In this 16th-century cartoon the devil is shown to be in control of Luther. The man with the musical instrument instead of a nose is meant to be Luther.

Martin Luther heard about what was going on. He could do little to stop it as long as he was in Wartburg Castle. He was very worried by the news. He was afraid that what he had started was getting out of control. There had always been people who wanted to smash the Roman Catholic Church. Luther was not one of these revolutionaries. He wanted to gradually change the Church to make it better. When he heard what was going on in Wittenberg he thought that the changes were going too far and too fast.

Luther was not the only one worried by the situation. Many wealthy and powerful people who supported him were also concerned. They knew that some of the revolutionaries wanted to change more than the Church. For them, changing the Church was just the beginning. They also wanted to change the way in which the country was run. Some wanted to take power and wealth away from the rich. This was not a popular idea with the wealthy people in Saxony.

In 1522 Luther left Wartburg Castle and returned to Wittenberg. He was determined to take control again and stop those who had acted while he was away. Luther wanted to change the things that he thought were very wrong in the Church. He did not want to change everything. Nor did he want the changes to cause violence and upheaval.

Between 1524 and 1525 his worst fears seemed to be proved right. Many thousands of **peasants** rose in revolt against the wealthy landowners. Luther was afraid that his ideas would get linked to this rebellion. He did all he could to show that he did not support the peasants. He encouraged the German rulers to crush the revolt.

Many other people were now having second thoughts about the ideas of the radical reformers. They were afraid that the Church and Germany were breaking apart. By 1525 the writer Erasmus no longer supported Luther. Luther also argued with another reformer named **Zwingli**. They could not agree about **Holy Communion**.

In 1529 the Emperor met with the rulers of the Empire at the **Diet of Speyer**. He threatened to use force against the people in Germany who supported Luther. Some German princes thought this was wrong. They protested to the Emperor. After this the supporters of Luther were called **Protestants**.

Melanchthon

Philip Melanchthon (1497–1560) was born in Bretten, modern Germany. He was a Humanist writer and theologian who supported Luther in his reform of the Church. He was educated at the universities of Heidelberg and Tübingen and became professor of Greek at Wittenberg in 1518.

By 1519 Melanchthon was defending Luther's views. He married in 1520. He led the Lutherans after Luther's death in 1546. He also reorganized education in Germany and reformed several universities.

3.3 The Reformation Survives

In 1530 the leaders of the Holy Roman Empire met once more. This time it was at the **Diet of Augsburg**. Luther could not attend because he had been condemned as an outlaw.

At this meeting it became clear that Emperor Charles V wanted to stop the spread of Protestant ideas. However, he also had other things on his mind. In 1529 Turkish armies had advanced as far as Vienna. The Empire was under threat. The Emperor would have to fight the Turks before facing the problem with the Protestants. The French were also keen to stir up trouble for the Emperor. They encouraged the German Protestants.

In 1531 the Protestant German princes joined together to defend each other. This **alliance** was known as the **Schmalkald League**. The states which joined included **Brandenburg, Prussia, Saxony, Hesse, Mansfeld, Brunswick, Anhalt** and twenty cities. Germany was being split by the ideas of Luther and by the wish of some of the rulers to have more freedom.

B **SOURCE**

The Emperor could do little. Affairs in Spain, in Africa, in Italy and in the Netherlands were for him more urgent. Only once in that critical period of twenty years (1521–41) did this king show himself among his German subjects. So, without serious interference the Lutheran faith spread through northern Germany.

From 'A History of Europe' by H. A. L. Fisher, 1935.

A copy of the Schmalkald Treaty, renewed in 1536.

A **SOURCE**

The Emperor could not stop them. The Turks advanced again in 1532 and the Emperor was also at war with France. He had fallen out with the Pope, too. In 1527 his soldiers had captured Rome and seized the Pope. The Protestants agreed to help him fight his wars if he left them to practise their religion.

Between 1536 and 1538 the Emperor did badly in his war with the French. In 1539 there was a revolt against his rule in the Netherlands. These difficulties in the Empire protected the German Protestants from being attacked.

In 1541 at the **Diet of Regensburg** any last hopes of peace between the Roman Catholics and Protestants ended. But once again the Emperor could not act. Between 1541 and 1547 he was at war with the Turks again. Also between 1542 and 1544 he was at war with France. He had much to concern him.

Martin Luther died in 1546. At last the Emperor was ready to take action against the Protestants. He persuaded the French to keep out of his quarrel with the Germans. He encouraged disagreements between the German states. The Emperor brought in extra soldiers from his lands in Italy and the Netherlands. In 1547 he finally defeated a Protestant army at the battle of **Mühlberg**.

However, the Emperor was not able to put an end to Protestantism. Some Protestant princes had supported him in the wars against France, and he did not want to attack them. Also, a disagreement broke out between the Emperor and his brother **Ferdinand**. Once more the Emperor had a lot to distract him.

The Protestant prince **Maurice of Saxony** made the most of this. He had supported the Emperor while he crushed rival Protestant states in 1547. Now Maurice broke the friendship. He did this to make Saxony strong as well as to protect Luther's ideas.

Maurice of Saxony persuaded the French king **Henry II** to support him. He also counted on the fact that the Emperor was old and tired. He forced the Emperor to agree to the **Treaty of Passau** (about 1552). This gave Protestant states the right to exist. Another treaty, the **Peace of Augsburg** in 1555, ended the civil war in Germany.

SOURCE C

I do not want to struggle for the Gospel [the 'Good News' about faith in Jesus] by violence and by murder.

From a letter sent by Martin Luther to a friend in the early 1530s.

Maurice of Saxony

Maurice of Saxony (1521–53) helped the Catholic Emperor Charles V in his battles against the Turks and French in the 1540s. Charles promised to make him Elector of Saxony so he refused to side with the Protestant princes fighting the Emperor.

He became elector after the defeat of the Protestants at Mühlberg in 1547. But soon he began to oppose Charles' plan to impose the Catholic religion on Germany. Also Charles refused to free Maurice's father-in-law from prison. In 1550 he allied himself with the French and Protestant princes, and defeated Charles in 1552.

3.4 The Reformation Spreads

The ideas of Martin Luther spread to many other countries in Europe. Luther's ideas were not new. In many countries people had been saying similar things for a long time. The success of the Protestants in Germany encouraged these people.

In Germany the followers of Luther became known as **Lutherans**. In other countries though, not everyone agreed with everything Luther said. Even in Germany there were many people who accepted some of his views but not all of them. This is important to remember. Even though the revolt against the power of the Pope spread, it did not mean that Luther was in control of it. He was not.

Protestant ideas had spread to **Switzerland** by 1518. By 1524 there were Protestant groups in the **Netherlands** and **Hungary**. In **Sweden** the Protestants had taken over the Church by 1527. The same thing happened in **Denmark** and in **Norway** in the 1530s. There were active Protestants in **France** by the 1550s and in **Scotland** by 1560. In Scotland they were led by **John Knox**. By 1552 Protestants had won enough followers among the landowners in **Poland** to stop the government from carrying out the orders of the Roman Catholic Church.

In **England**, matters were more complicated. **Henry VIII** (reigned 1509–47) was against the power of the Pope but made no effort to change the basic beliefs of the Church. During the reign of his son, **Edward VI** (reigned 1547–53), Protestants became more powerful. When Edward died his step-sister **Mary** became queen (reigned 1553–58). She was a devout Roman Catholic. Mary had many Protestants tortured and executed during her reign. She was followed by **Queen Elizabeth I** (reigned 1558–1603) who encouraged Protestantism but did not go as far in changing the Church as some Protestants wanted.

People supported the Reformation for different reasons. We call this having different **motives**. In countries like **Sweden** and **Denmark**, the Reformation was quick and without violence. Here the rulers encouraged the changes. In some countries like **France** and the **Netherlands**, there was a lot of bloodshed. Here the rulers opposed the changes. In **Poland** many landowners supported the Reformation. It was easier for them to do so as they had great power. For years some of the **nobles** had disagreed with the king and the Roman Catholic Church.

A SOURCE

At the Diet of Augsburg (1530) the Protestant princes attended Lutheran services. The Emperor demanded that it should cease. 'Sir,' said the old Margrave of Brandenburg-Ansbach, 'rather than that I should leave off the Word of God, I would kneel here on the spot and lose my head.' Badly taken aback Charles could only stammer, in his broken German: 'My dear lords, no heads off.'

From 'Reformation Europe' by G. Elton, 1963.

B SOURCE

In England a unique relationship arose almost by accident. Henry VIII became entangled with the Pope over his wish to dissolve one of his six marriages in order to remarry and get an heir. With the support of his Parliament, Henry proclaimed himself head of the Church in England and opened the way to the development of an English Church separate from Rome.

From 'History of the World' by J. Roberts, 1980.

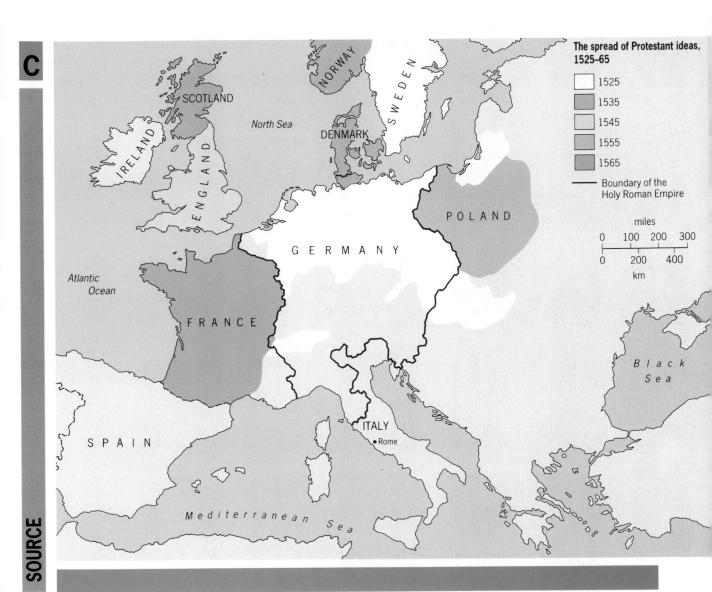

The spread of Protestant ideas, 1525–65

- 1525
- 1535
- 1545
- 1555
- 1565
- Boundary of the Holy Roman Empire

NORWAY

SWEDEN

SCOTLAND

North Sea

DENMARK

IRELAND

ENGLAND

POLAND

Atlantic Ocean

GERMANY

FRANCE

Black Sea

SPAIN

ITALY
• Rome

Mediterranean Sea

miles
0   100   200   300

0   200   400
km

D

The power of the local lord was much more real than that of the distant king.

A. Maczak describing the situation in Poland in the mid-16th century. From 'Politics and Society in Reformation Europe', 1987.

Frederick I

Frederick I of Denmark (1471–1533) encouraged the spread of Lutheran ideas in Denmark while keeping a balance between the opposing Lutheran and Catholic nobles in order to keep in power. In 1523 he became King of Denmark, following a revolt of the nobles against King Christian II, who was Frederick's nephew. As the new king, he wanted the support of both the nobles and the Danish peasants. In 1524 he also became King of Norway. At first he supported the Catholic Danish nobles in opposing Lutheran ideas, but he then began to support Lutheran preachers working in Denmark. This made Frederick more popular with the peasants and increased his power over the Danish Church. He defeated attempts to overthrow him and made peace with Emperor Charles V.

3.5 The Peasants' War

In Germany in the early 16th century, there was a lot of unrest among the **peasants**. Peasants were people who owned small farms. They were hard working. They were becoming more confident and wanted to get rid of anything which stopped them from getting the most out of their farms.

During the **Middle Ages** the peasants had been part of the **feudal system**. This meant that their land was controlled by a local lord. Peasants were often forced to do work for their local lord. They had to pay taxes. They had to use the lord's mill. They had to get the lord's permission if they wanted to move to another village. The peasants wanted to put an end to this system. They were helped by the fact that Germany was so divided that the lords could not unite against them. But this was beginning to change. In different parts of Germany, the lords were trying to bring the peasants under their control once more. This led to trouble.

Peasants looting the Abbey of Weissenau, drawn by Abbot Murer in 1525.

SOURCE B

At the same time, greater burdens than ever were imposed upon the only class of the population which did any really useful work.

From 'Government in Reformation Europe' by W. Hubatsch, 1971.

SOURCE C

The times are so unusual that a prince might get to heaven more easily by killing people than by praying.

Advice from Luther to the lords, in 'Against the Murdering Plundering Hordes of Peasants', 1525.

SOURCE A

In the mid-1470s there was a peasant rebellion in the German state of Würzburg. Here, **Hans Böhm** claimed to have seen visions from God. He claimed that peasants should no longer pay taxes, or give a **tithe** (one-tenth of their crops), to the Church. This idea was very popular with the peasants, but it frightened the lords. Böhm's ideas spread across south and central Germany. Eventually he was arrested and burned.

There were more peasant revolts in the **Rhineland** in 1502, 1513 and 1517. Here the peasants marched under a flag which was decorated with a peasant's clog. They took their name from the German word for this type of shoe: **Bundschuh**. Some of the demonstrations started with simple protests and turned into open revolts which were crushed by the lords.

In 1524 a great peasant revolt swept southern Germany. This happened at the same time as the ideas of the Reformation were beginning to spread. Until 1525 the revolt was not very violent. Most of the peasants only wanted to protect their rights. However, the lords wanted to crush the peasants and caused massacres in many parts of Germany. Approximately 100,000 men and women were slaughtered.

Martin Luther feared that if there were a bloody revolution his Reformation ideas would be lost. In 1525 he wrote a booklet, **Admonition to Peace**. In this booklet he advised the lords to carry out some of the reforms which the peasants wanted. When the peasants' complaints turned into pitched battles, Luther condemned them. In another booklet, **Against the Murdering Plundering Hordes of Peasants**, he advised the lords to smash the peasant revolt.

Some historians feel that Luther encouraged the lords to act with terrible savagery. His last booklet caused him to lose the support of the peasants of southern Germany. They would not forget how he had encouraged the lords to crush them and to destroy their freedom.

At the end of the revolt some of the most violent acts took place in a part of Germany called **Thuringia**. Here **Thomas Müntzer** (1490–1525) encouraged the peasants and workers to attack castles and burn churches. This violence has influenced many later historians' views of the revolt. But in most parts of Germany the peasants acted in an orderly way. It was the lords who turned the revolt into a series of bloody massacres.

D **SOURCE**

In what was the only popular revolt in German history, Luther advised the princes to adopt the most ruthless measures against the 'mad dogs', as he called the desperate, downtrodden peasants. Luther employed a brutality of language unequalled until the Nazi time.

From 'The Rise and Fall of the Third Reich' by W. Shirer, 1964.

Müntzer

Thomas Müntzer (1490–1525) differed from Luther in that he believed each person could decide for themselves what is God's will, rather than relying on the Bible. Müntzer studied at the universities at Leipzig and Frankfurt, in modern Germany.

From 1513–18 he was a clergyman and teacher. His last teaching job was at Frohse monastery where he supported Luther. By 1520, while he was studying at the monastery of Beuditz, he decided that the ideas of the Reformation should lead to revolution. Expelled from the town of Zwickau in 1521, he eventually broke away from Luther in 1522. In 1523 he moved to Allstedt and then Mühlhausen, organizing working people to revolt against their masters. He was executed in 1525.

3.6 Life in the New German Churches

Martin Luther did not intend to start a new Church. He wanted to reform the one he was in. However, as we have seen, the Roman Catholic Church was split by his actions. In some places his ideas were put into practice. In other places they were rejected.

One of the places in which his ideas were eventually accepted was in northern Germany. Here, the churches which refused to accept the authority of the Pope were called **Lutheran**.

The beliefs of the Lutheran Protestants were set down in the **Confession of Augsburg** of 1530. Luther disagreed with many things done by the Roman Catholics, but he only wanted to change what he felt was absolutely necessary. If a way of doing something was not actually banned in the **New Testament**, Luther was willing for it to take place in one of his churches. He was also very keen to work with the German princes. Those who agreed with him he called **'Godly princes'**.

Part of a wall painting from a Lutheran church in Germany. It was painted in 1617. This section shows some of the main beliefs of the Lutheran churches.

Martin Luther was a powerful speaker and leader, but he was not a great organizer. However, as it became obvious that the Lutheran churches were going to split from the Roman Catholic Church, he worked hard to replace the old Roman Catholic ideas. In 1526 Luther wrote **Orders of Service** for the German Lutheran churches. These explained how a church service should be run. In 1529 he wrote the **Shorter Catechism**, which explained exactly what Lutherans believed.

Each of the Lutheran churches was run by a group of people called the **consistory**. The first consistory was set up by **John Frederick of Saxony** in 1539. It was responsible for what happened in the Church. The consistory was controlled by the local lord. Some German Christians felt that this situation was not much better than when the Church had been run by the Pope. They argued that the members of the Church should be able to elect their own leaders.

In the new Lutheran churches, **preaching** was a very important part of the church service. The preacher read the Bible and explained what it had to say. For Lutherans, the Bible was the only trustworthy way to find out about God and how they should live their lives. The Lutheran preachers explained that people got to heaven not by being good enough but by believing in God only. This was called **Justification by Faith**. Lutherans rejected any beliefs which were not found in the Bible.

In the Lutheran churches, **hymns** were sung in German instead of in Latin. Ministers of the Church were allowed to marry. In 1525 Luther married Catherine von Bora. She had once been a nun. Roman Catholic priests could not marry. Luther also believed that ordinary people should be given both bread and wine at Communion. In the Roman Catholic Church, ordinary people were just given bread; only the priests were given bread and wine.

John Frederick I

John Frederick I (1503–54), known as 'the Magnanimous' (generous, fair), was one of the rulers who Lutherans described as 'Godly princes'. This meant they supported and encouraged the ideas of the Protestants. These rulers sometimes did so for a mix of different reasons. It was their support for the new ideas which helped them survive.

John Frederick was born in Torgau, in modern Germany. He was the ruler, or Elector, of Saxony after 1532. He was head of the Schmalkald League – the group of German states who were in favour of the new Protestant ideas. He did not want to fight the Catholic Holy Roman Emperor Charles V, because he hoped that their disagreements could be settled peacefully.

However, John Frederick soon angered the Emperor. First, he forced the Catholic bishop of Naumburg to stand down in favour of a Protestant bishop. Second, he fell out with his second cousin, Duke Maurice, and seized the town of Wurzen from him. The first act angered the Emperor, and the second one divided the Protestant princes, since Maurice looked to the Emperor to help him. Charles V was angry at what John Frederick had done and was ready to use force against him. With the help of Duke Maurice, Charles defeated John Frederick and his allies at the battle of Mühlberg in 1547.

John Frederick was captured and sentenced to death. However, his life was spared when he finally accepted the loss of some of his lands and the fact that he could no longer be an elector (one of the princes with the power to vote for who would be Emperor). He did not surrender any of his religious beliefs, and it was not until 1552 that he was freed. He never again became Elector.

4.1 The Radical Reformation

Luther was not the only person preaching new ideas in the 1520s. Others were also questioning the right of the Pope. Historians sometimes call these people members of the **Radical Reformation**. They were far more revolutionary than Luther.

Some of these people were known as **Anabaptists**. This word describes many different groups of people. Although they were not part of one organization, they often shared some beliefs. For example, they all thought that only adults should be baptized and not children. This was because adults were able to say what they believed in. Many of them thought that it was wrong to use violence, and that no one should be *forced* to believe anything. Most also believed that members of a church should elect their own leaders and that Christians should live pure lives. Some of them went further and said that Christians should share all they owned with each other.

In 1525 Anabaptists led by **Conrad Grebel** met in Zürich. They were threatened by other Protestants in the city. The people against the Anabaptists did not want a revolution in the Church. One of the Anabaptist leaders, **Michael Sattler**, was burnt at the stake. He was killed by other Protestants, not Roman Catholics.

Soon, Anabaptist groups were springing up all over Germany. Some were started when the Swiss Anabaptists fled to Germany. The Anabaptist leader, **Balthasar Hubmaier**, had to escape to Moravia (in modern Czechoslovakia). He persuaded many people to join him. In 1528, he was burnt at the stake in Vienna. His wife was executed by drowning. They were killed by Roman Catholics.

The main Anabaptist beliefs.

Adults only should be baptized.

Anabaptists should not use violence if attacked.

Church members could vote and control how the Church was run.

Many Protestant leaders feared the revolutionary Anabaptists. Luther openly quarrelled with them in 1535. Roman Catholics and Protestants alike attacked them.

Two famous preachers accused of being Anabaptists were **Thomas Müntzer** (1489–1525) and **Niklas Storch**. They were not in favour of peace. They declared that the poor should destroy the rich.

Müntzer and Storch began to preach at Zwickau, Germany. Many of the town's silver miners supported them. There was a lot of unemployment around the town and prices were rising. Poorer people were insecure and frightened by this.

In 1521 they were **expelled** from Zwickau by the town authorities. They travelled and preached that the powerful rulers should be swept away. Many peasants supported them, as did the copper miners in a part of Germany called **Thuringia**. This was at the time of the Peasants' War (see Unit 3.5). Müntzer led a peasant uprising in 1525. He was condemned by Luther. An army led by the German princes crushed his revolution, killing 5,000 peasants and miners in a bloody massacre. Müntzer was beheaded.

Despite these setbacks, the Anabaptists remained popular among many poorer people. They were impressed by the faith and determination of the Anabaptists. They wanted to have a say in how their Church and country was run. The peasants felt betrayed by Luther who had supported the princes during the Peasants' War.

C SOURCE

1 No one can truly know Christ unless they obey him with their lives.
2 The Government defends the Word of God with a fist. This is wrong.

Anabaptist sayings from the mid-16th century.

Grebel

Conrad Grebel (1498–1526) was born in Zürich, in Switzerland. He was the chief leader of a group of Anabaptists called the Swiss Brethren. He was educated at Basle, Vienna and Paris. Grebel believed in non-violence.

At first Grebel supported the Swiss reformer Zwingli but then disagreed with him because, in Grebel's opinion, the reforms in the Church were happening too slowly. He also wanted to stop the government having power over the Church.

In 1524 Grebel helped set up an Anabaptist church in Zürich. In 1525 the city government ordered him to stop, because it disagreed with the Anabaptist belief that only adults should be baptized. He disobeyed them and in January 1525 carried out the first adult baptism in modern history.

All beliefs should come from the Bible.

Anabaptists would not use force to make people agree with them.

4.2 Münster, 1535

For almost 200 years after the 1520s the word 'Anabaptist' was used to describe any dangerous person who threatened to break up society. This was partly because Anabaptists refused to obey the government when it told them what they should believe. Government leaders were frightened that if people were free to choose their own religion they might soon want to choose their own government. Also some Anabaptists were very revolutionary. They led attacks on the way society was ruled. Perhaps the wildest and most famous attack took place in Münster, a city in north-western Germany.

Münster was ruled by a Roman Catholic bishop. Many people in the city were not happy about this. The priests did not pay taxes like other citizens. The bishop stopped the merchants from running the town in the way they wanted to. During the Peasants' War, the citizens forced the bishop to give them more power. When the war was over he broke these promises.

By 1532 there was also plague in the area. The harvests had been poor and taxes were increasing. People were unhappy. In 1532 supporters of Luther took control of the town. Many rich merchants supported them. The bishop was unable to stop the take-over.

The situation soon got out of control. Many poor people flooded into Münster. Most came from the Netherlands. Many were unemployed cloth workers. They were desperate and wanted change. One of these newcomers was **Jan of Leyden**, who was an Anabaptist and a revolutionary.

Jan of Leyden soon won the right for people in Münster to believe in what they wanted. This is called **liberty of conscience**. This attracted many other extreme Anabaptists to the city. The richer citizens were afraid and left the city. Churches were robbed. Jan proclaimed that God would soon destroy all the world, saving only Münster. Jan was joined by another Anabaptist leader, **Jan Matthys**.

In February 1534, the bishop tried to recapture the city. He surrounded it with soldiers. The **siege** lasted until June 1535. In the city anyone who disagreed with the Anabaptist leaders was killed. Money was banned. All food had to be shared. All books were destroyed, except the Bible.

SOURCE A

There is evidence to suggest that the unemployed were both more numerous and more desperate than in earlier centuries.

A description of the cloth workers in the Netherlands from 'The Pursuit of the Millenium' by N. Cohn, 1970.

SOURCE B

And so they came, the Dutch and the Frisians and scoundrels from all parts who had never settled anywhere. They flocked to Münster.

An eyewitness account of events in Münster, 1533.

SOURCE C

Slay all monks and priests, and all sovereigns in the world; since our king alone is the true sovereign.

War song of the Münster Anabaptists, 1535. The king was Jan of Leyden.

SOURCE

The execution of Jan of Leyden, from a 16th-century German print. He was first led on a chain through nearby towns, then tortured to death with red-hot irons. His body was hung in a cage to rot. The cage is still in the church at Münster.

At Easter 1534, Jan Matthys was killed in a battle. He had gone to battle with only a few people because he thought that God had told him to do this. Jan of Leyden announced that he was **King of the New Jerusalem**. He lived in luxury. Jan had fifteen wives. He killed anyone who disagreed with him, and women who argued with their husbands were executed. Jan promised the citizens that the cobblestones would turn to bread. They did not and the people starved.

At last the bishop's soldiers succeeded in getting into the city. Jan of Leyden was captured and executed in January 1536. The bishop had him tortured with red-hot irons. Jan died without making a sound.

The Anabaptists at Münster were different from most Anabaptists. Most Anabaptists would not use violence. They would not force people to do something. But for years, the events in Münster affected how people thought about Anabaptists.

Hoffmann

Melchior Hoffmann (1495–1544) was born in modern Germany. He worked as a Lutheran preacher in modern Latvia, Estonia, Sweden and north Germany. In 1529 he was banned from Denmark because his beliefs were different from Luther's. Hoffmann preached that the world would end in 1533 and that he and Christ would set up a government together in Strassburg. Hoffmann was imprisoned and died in 1544. Many of the Dutch Anabaptists at Münster were followers of his beliefs.

4.3 The Peaceful Revolutionaries

Most Anabaptists were not violent. They wanted to live peaceful lives. After the terrible things that happened at Münster, many rejected all violence.

One of the leaders of these peaceful Anabaptists was **Menno Simmons** (1496–1561). He had been a Roman Catholic priest in the part of the Netherlands known as **Friesland**. In 1536 he left the Roman Catholic Church and became a travelling preacher.

The people who accepted his ideas are called **brethren** or **Mennonites**. Mennonites were Christians who refused to use any kind of violence, following the teachings of Jesus. They thought that local groups of Christians should run their own affairs. They also thought that Christians should not get involved in politics. In their services they washed one another's feet. This reminded them that like Jesus they had to love and care for each other. They greeted each other with a **kiss of peace**.

Menno Simmons (1496–1561).

A Hutterite family, 1589.

A SOURCE

If anyone disobeyed these ideas they were punished by being **shunned**. This meant that no other Mennonite would have anything to do with them. In Germany and the Netherlands, there was a split in the Mennonite movement. This was about how strict punishments should be for anyone who broke the rules. The strictest Mennonites totally ignored those who broke the rules.

Other peaceful Anabaptists were to be found in southern Germany and in modern Czechoslovakia. These were led by **Jorg Cajob**. Many had escaped from **persecution** in the 1520s. At this time, many Anabaptists had been killed because of their beliefs.

These Anabaptists lived together in a **Brüderhof**. In English this means 'brotherhouse'. All the families in a Brüderhof shared what they owned or earned with the other families. These people came to be called **Hutterites** in the 1530s, after one of their leaders, **Jakob Hutter**.

The Hutterites tried to make everything that their little communities needed. This is called being **self-sufficient**. By the early 17th century, they had a reputation as being honest and peaceful craftworkers. They became famous as **doctors**, **clock makers** and **furniture makers**.

In the 1620s a fierce war began in Europe. It was called the **Thirty Years War**. During this war Roman Catholic soldiers destroyed the peaceful Hutterite communities. The survivors fled to the Turkish lands.

C **SOURCE**

Private property is the greatest enemy of love. The true Christian must get free from owning property, if they want to become a disciple [of Jesus].

Extract from a Hutterite leaflet from 1545.

D **SOURCE**

We think that it is wrong to buy something and sell it to make a profit. This makes the thing more expensive to poor people. To do this takes the bread from their mouths.

Extract from a Hutterite leaflet from about 1540.

Simmons

Menno Simmons (1496–1561) was born at Witmarsum, in Friesland, in the modern Netherlands. This former Catholic priest became an important Anabaptist leader and a believer in pacifism, or non-violence.

He became a priest in 1524 at Utrecht, in the Netherlands. He soon began to have doubts about Catholic beliefs about both Holy Communion and infant baptism. In January 1536 he left his parish and went into hiding to rethink his beliefs.

By early 1537 he decided that Christians should be baptized as adults and was rebaptized. He joined a group of Anabaptists, formed by Obbe Philips, soon became their leader, and married. Both the Catholic and Lutheran Churches regarded him as a heretic. In constant danger, he travelled and preached in East Friesland, 1543–4, and worked in the Rhineland, 1544–6. He set up his headquarters near Oldesloe (in Holstein, in modern Germany). He died there in 1561.

5.1 Crisis in Switzerland

At about the time that Luther was beginning the Reformation in Germany, changes were also happening in **Switzerland**. In this country the person who began the changes was **Huldreich Zwingli** (1484–1531).

Zwingli studied in the Swiss cities of **Basle** and **Berne**. He became **vicar** of the church in the city of **Glarus**. He was also the **chaplain** to one of the Swiss armies. This meant that he took care of the religious needs of the soldiers. These soldiers would fight for whoever paid them. They were called **mercenaries**. As their chaplain, Zwingli was present at two battles.

Zwingli was very **patriotic**. This means that he was very proud of his country. He wanted the Swiss to be free from the rule of other countries.

In Germany, Luther at first did not want to break away from the Roman Catholic Church. In Switzerland, Zwingli wanted a complete break.

B

SOURCE

They were too democratic to be easily handled. The Swiss were as poverty stricken as they were liberty loving.

From 'Crisis in Europe', by V. Kiernan, 1965. This extract describes how the people of Switzerland were poor, but loved freedom.

C

SOURCE

When he [Luther] heard of Zwingli's death on the battlefield, he commented: 'I sorrow for Zwingli, because I have little hope for him [going to heaven]'.

From 'Luther the Reformer' by J. Kittelson, 1989.

Religious divisions in Switzerland at the time of Zwingli's death, 1531.

A

SOURCE

- Protestants
- Catholics

Zwingli met **Erasmus** in 1515. He was impressed with Erasmus' ideas. In 1518 Zwingli became priest at the **Great Minster**, in **Zürich**, where he began his reforms. Like Luther he worked with the people who ran the city. In 1522 he married **Anna Meyer**.

In 1523 there was a great debate between Zwingli and the Roman Catholic **Bishop of Constance**. Zwingli explained his beliefs. They were that a person only got to heaven through faith in God; the Bible was the only sure way to find out about God; and that ministers of the Church should be able to marry.

The town council of Zürich heard Zwingli defend his ideas. They decided that he was right. They allowed priests and monks to have wives. Anything done in the churches which was not taught in the Bible they banned.

In 1528 Zwingli took part in another debate. This time it was in **Berne**. After he explained his ideas, the Swiss cities of **Basle**, **Gall**, **Schaffhausen** and **Constance** joined him.

In 1529 Zwingli and Luther had a disagreement. At the **Conference of Marburg** they could not agree about what they believed about Holy Communion. They could not overcome their differences. As a result, the German princes would not support Zwingli's Reformation. Instead they supported Luther.

Zwingli was very different from Luther. He did not respect history the way Luther did. Zwingli wanted to change the Church in many ways. In Zürich, organs, pictures and statues were removed from churches. This was because Zwingli thought they were wrong and distracted people from the worship of God. Church services became very simple. Everything that happened in a service had to be mentioned in the Bible.

Not everyone in Switzerland agreed with Zwingli. Some people preferred to stay Roman Catholic. The Roman Catholic areas of the county were called the **Forest Cantons**. The Forest Cantons sent an army to attack Zürich. In 1531 Zwingli died fighting for his ideas at the battle of **Kappel**. As a result of this battle, the different areas of Switzerland were left to choose their own beliefs. The country was divided.

Heinrich Bullinger (1504–75) became the next leader of the Swiss Reformation. In 1549 the Protestants who followed Bullinger united with other Protestants living in Geneva.

D

SOURCE

The change of appearance and worship in the Swiss churches was more revolutionary than in the churches of northern Germany.

From 'The Reformation' by O. Chadwick, 1972.

Bullinger

Heinrich Bullinger (1504–75) was born in Bremgarten, in Switzerland. He studied at the University of Cologne, in modern Germany, where he agreed with the ideas of men like Luther. In 1528 Bullinger supported Zwingli, and in 1530 he became a Protestant minister at Bremgarten.

After Zwingli was killed in battle, Bullinger took over as minister of the Protestants of Zürich. He wrote letters to foreign rulers such as Henry VIII and Edward VI of England and Francis II of France, explaining his religious ideas. He was unable to heal the split with Luther that had happened under Zwingli's leadership but he did reach agreement with Calvin.

5.2 John Calvin at Geneva

The death of Zwingli at the battle of Kappel stopped the growth of Reformation ideas in Switzerland and its region. But from 1536, changes began again. This time they were started by a Frenchman, **John Calvin** (1509–64).

Calvin had first come across the ideas of Martin Luther while he was a student in Paris. In 1533, after much thought, he finally left the Roman Catholic Church. He went to the Swiss city of **Basle**. Many other French people lived in this city. Here he wrote a book which explained his ideas about God. It is called ***The Institution of the Christian Religion***. It is usually called, for short, ***The Institutes***.

Calvin's ideas had a tremendous impact on many people. Like Luther and Zwingli he believed that when Christians wanted to know about God, they should turn to the Bible and not the Pope. He also believed that people could only experience God if God chose to show Himself to them.

Calvin believed that men and women were unfit for heaven. He believed that their very nature was **sinful**. At the beginning of time God had decided that some people were going to go to heaven. The rest were going to hell. Who went to heaven was God's decision. It had nothing to do with the actions or ideas of the people. This belief is called **predestination**.

B Good-bye Geneva. In the end the King of France himself will be a citizen here.

A comment by one of the enemies of Calvin, in the 1550s.

C SOURCE The easy-going unstable city of the past emerged as a grim, solid community of psalm-singing church go-ers. Calvin's Geneva should be treated seriously as an awful warning.

From 'Reformation Europe' by G. Elton, 1963.

D If he once gets his knife into you, you do not stand a chance.

Comment by one of the other Church leaders in Geneva in the 1550s. It describes the way in which Calvin dealt with people who disagreed with him.

A SOURCE

A sketch of Calvin drawn by one of his students during a lecture. It dates from the 1550s.

In 1536 Calvin was invited to live in **Geneva**. The leader of the Reformation there was **Guillaume Farel**. He asked Calvin to help him. But Calvin was not popular in Geneva and was forced to leave. Many Swiss people disliked being told what to believe by a foreigner. In 1541 he was invited to go back. Even then many people were not happy. It was not until 1555 that he was finally in control of the Church in the city.

Calvin wanted to make Geneva a **city of God**, where everything was run the way Calvin and his supporters thought was right. The city laws were changed to stop sinful behaviour. Calvin tried to make sure that the Church controlled the lives of all the citizens. In Geneva, Calvin's Church often clashed with the government.

Geneva became the home to many people whose beliefs had been banned in their own countries. They came to Geneva because they agreed with Calvin. A school was set up to teach **theology**. This is the study of God and ideas about God. The school was called the **Geneva Academy**. Calvin set out his ideas in a more orderly way than Luther did. Also, unlike Luther, he always thought out carefully what he was going to say, write and do.

It was the most perfect school of Christ that there ever was on earth, since the days of the apostles [the first followers of Jesus].

John Knox, the leader of the Reformation in Scotland, commenting on the Geneva Academy in the 1560s.

A portrait of Calvin.

Knox

John Knox (1514–72) was born in East Lothian, in Scotland. He was the leader of the Reformation in Scotland. He made the churches there both strict and democratic. After studying at the University of St Andrews he became a priest and was a tutor to a Scottish Protestant family.

Knox was impressed by the ideas of George Wishart who was burned for heresy in 1546. Knox was imprisoned and spent 19 months as a slave of the French. Living for a time in England, he was forced to flee when Mary Tudor became queen. He returned to Scotland in 1559 to lead the Reformation there.

5.3 Life in Geneva

John Calvin's ideas affected the way that people lived in the city of Geneva. He believed that the Church should carefully control the lives of the citizens. This would stop wrong things from being done. Problems arose because not everyone agreed with him about what was wrong.

Calvin's church was well-organized. In 1541 he laid down how it should be run. This was explained in his **Ecclesiastic Ordinances**. Ecclesiastic is another word for 'church'. Ordinances means 'rules'.

The rules stated that there were four different leaders in the Church. Some were called **pastors**. Their job was to preach and control the Church. Some were called **teachers**. Their job was to make sure that people believed the right things. Some were called **deacons**. Their job was to look after the poor. All these jobs were done by men. People who are not full-time ministers are called **lay people**. Some lay people could become **elders**. The elders helped to run the Church. This kind of organization is known as a **Presbyterian Church**. The leaders met together every Thursday in a group called a **consistory**.

Calvin's idea of the Church was not **democratic**. The ordinary people did not run the Church. Pastors were chosen by other pastors and not by the people. The elders of the Church in Geneva tried to make sure people behaved properly. This was not a new practice. The old Roman Catholic bishops had also tried to control the way people lived.

Between 1541 and 1546 in Geneva, 58 people were executed for disagreeing with the Church. A further 76 were thrown out of the city. In 1546 taverns (modern pubs) were made illegal. In 1547 it was made illegal to wear fashionable trousers. A law against dancing was passed in 1550. The pastors were given the right to visit every home in Geneva, to make sure that people were living the way they had been told.

However, Calvin did not have total control. The **City Council** had the power to stop a man becoming a pastor. People could only be executed or expelled if the council agreed. Despite Calvin's complaints, taverns were reopened. An attempt to force people to have only Biblical names was also rejected by the council. The council complained if the pastors preached for too long.

A **SOURCE**

The way things are organized does not mean that the pastors have any power in the Government.

The Church does not have the authority to interfere with magistrates and the courts.

Church rules of Geneva in the 1540s.

B **SOURCE**

They thought of themselves as responsible for the protection of old people, orphans, widows, children, the sick.

From 'The Reformation' by O. Chadwick, 1972.

C **SOURCE**

We are like dogs, who bark when our master is attacked.

A comment made by a member of the Church consistory of Geneva in the 1540s.

Some members of the council were also members of the Church consistory. This suggests that Calvin only succeeded because enough important people in Geneva supported what he was doing.

Calvin was also helped by the many French people who fled to Geneva. They had been punished for their beliefs in France. In Geneva they supported the changes brought about by Calvin.

Someone said that the arrival of the French refugees put up the cost of living. A woman tried to cure her husband by tying round his neck a walnut containing a spider. Another danced. A woman of 62 married a man of 25.

Complaints about some Geneva citizens discussed by the consistory on 16 February, 1542.

Some of the changes Calvin brought to churches in Geneva:

- Anything not mentioned in the Bible was banned from church services.
- Simple churches. No ornaments or statues. No robes for the pastors.
- Members took Holy Communion around a table. There was no altar.
- Congregations sang hymns but they were not accompanied by musical instruments.

Farel

Guillaume Farel (1489–1565) was originally from Dauphine, in modern France. This Protestant preacher was the first person to introduce the ideas of the Reformation to the French speaking areas of Switzerland successfully.

Farel had become a Protestant by 1521 but was impatient with the slow way that changes were happening in the French Church. When Protestants began to be persecuted, he fled from Paris to Basle in Switzerland. After a great disagreement there with Erasmus he was forced to move on, eventually settling in Geneva in 1532.

By the time that the citizens of Geneva decided to follow the new Protestant ideas in 1536, Farel had become the leader of the new movement. It was Farel who persuaded Calvin to settle in Geneva in 1536 as his assistant. By 1538 Calvin was beginning to replace Farel as leader of the Protestants of Geneva.

Farel was a famous and striking preacher. He was widely respected by other preachers and reformers, and he had a great influence on Calvin.

6.1 The Council of Trent

When Martin Luther first started to complain about the Roman Catholic Church the Pope did not realize how serious it was going to be. **Pope Leo X** had other things on his mind: he was involved in politics, he was keen on hunting and gambling, and he spent a lot of time and money buying works of art. He hoped to get rid of Luther without much bother. He was wrong.

By 1520 the leaders of the Roman Catholic Church were beginning to realize they had made a mistake. Luther was not going to go away. He had become famous. The Church was splitting apart.

Some Roman Catholics realized there were problems in the Church. In 1517 a society called the **Oratory of Divine Love** was started in Rome. Its leaders were Roman Catholics who thought that some things should change in the Church. One of its members was **Gasparo Contarini**. He was born in 1483 and became a **cardinal** in 1535. A cardinal is a high-ranking person in the Roman Catholic Church.

A comment made by Pope Leo X in 1518.

The Council of Trent (1563).

A

SOURCE

Contarini was a peacemaker. He tried to heal the split with the Lutherans. In Italy some Roman Catholics called him a traitor. He failed to bring the two sides together.

People such as Contarini believed that the Roman Catholic Church had to change. If it did not change, other people would follow Luther and leave the Church. If it were to survive, the Roman Catholic Church would have to show that it could improve itself. This attempt to improve the Roman Catholic Church is known as the **Counter Reformation**.

In 1523 Clement VII (Leo X's brother) became Pope. He tried to reform the Church but found it was not easy. He could not get the Roman Catholic King of France and the Roman Catholic Holy Roman Emperor to agree with one another. They were bitter rivals. This situation made it hard to unite the Church.

In 1534 Pope Clement died and was replaced by Pope Paul III. He tried to stop **bribery** in the Church. He tried to make people obey **Church laws**. He tried to make **monks** live holier lives. He tried to ban **prostitutes** from the city of Rome.

Pope Paul was only successful with a few of these reforms. However, he did do something very important. He called together a great meeting of the Roman Catholic Church. It was called the **Council of Trent**.

The Council met in the city of Trent in northern Italy. It had three meetings: 1545–47, 1551–52 and 1562–63. Most of the people who came were from Italy, Spain and the lands of the Holy Roman Empire. Even some Protestants attended. In 1552, when they saw they could not agree with the Roman Catholics, they left.

The Council of Trent made it clear that none of Luther's basic points would be listened to. Indulgences could no longer be sold, but were still seen as good and useful. The Pope was still going to be the head of the Church. The Roman Catholic Church still taught that people could get to heaven by what they did as well as by what they believed. The Protestant ideas (**doctrines**) were rejected. The Pope was stronger than ever. Roman Catholic ideas were being defended and publicized.

SOURCE C

The Roman Catholic Church seemed to be unaware of the widespread unrest among the faithful, which Luther's protest represented.

From 'History of Christianity' by R. Linder, 1990.

Charles V

Charles V (1500–58), born in Ghent, in modern Belgium, was King of Spain from 1516 and Holy Roman Emperor after 1519. He tried to keep the Empire united but failed to do so, faced with Protestant German princes who would no longer obey him, attacks from the Muslim Turks and bitter rivalry with the Catholic King of France. He even faced opposition from the Pope.

All of these problems made it difficult for the Catholic Church to unite against the Protestants. It was these problems and the growing strength of the Protestants which led to the Pope calling together the Council of Trent.

In 1529 Charles defeated the League of Cognac, which the Pope had formed against him. He defeated the German Protestants in 1547. However, when the French supported the German princes in 1551, Charles' empire was shattered. He gave up his crown to his son in 1555–6 and died in 1558.

6.2 The Inquisition

Many people who opposed the Roman Catholic Church found themselves facing the **Inquisition**. This was a special type of court. Most courts only examine a person's **actions**. In the Inquisition courts, the judges also tried to judge the thoughts in a person's mind. Their aim was to find and punish people who disagreed with the Roman Catholic Church and its leaders.

The Inquisition was not started just to get rid of Protestants. It had existed for many years. Its official name was the **Supreme Sacred Congregation of the Holy Office**. It used torture to get information and employed secret agents. After 1224, people found guilty by the Inquisition could be executed by the rulers of the country in which the trial had taken place.

Many of the leading members of the Inquisition were from the **Dominican** order of monks. It was the Dominicans who had led the opposition to Martin Luther in Germany. They would have sentenced him to be burned, if they had been able to catch him.

People who disagreed with the Church were accused of being **heretics**. If two witnesses accused someone of being a heretic, that person would be arrested. Often the person was not told the charge or who had made the accusation. Any lawyer who tried to defend the accused person was likely to be arrested as well. Trials often lasted a long time. During this time the accused person was kept in prison.

People found **guilty** of being heretics were punished in different ways. The least serious punishments were to go on a **pilgrimage** or to go to a certain number of **church services**.

B SOURCE

Even if my own father were a heretic, I would gather wood to burn him.

A comment made by Pope Paul IV in the 1550s.

A SOURCE

Those found guilty of more serious 'crimes' were **whipped**. Others were **fined** or had their property **confiscated**. If a person refused to give up his or her beliefs, they would be **executed**. Often they were **burnt at the stake**. This was done by the local representatives of the ruler of the country. The Church did not actually do the killing.

During the Reformation many people turned against the Pope. The Inquisition was very active after 1541. In Roman Catholic countries it was used to prevent people from turning against the Roman Catholic Church. The Inquisition was led by a man named **Cardinal Caraffa** who later became Pope Paul IV. The Inquisition was most powerful where most of the population was Roman Catholic. It found it difficult to work in places where many people were Protestants, or if the ruler were sympathetic to Protestants. It did most of its work in **Italy**, **Spain** and **France**. Some rulers used the Inquisition to get rid of people they did not like. In Spain and France the rulers had a lot of control over the actions of the Inquisition. Sometimes, however, it was more complicated. In 1547 King Henry II of France wanted to use the Inquisition. The French parliament would not let him. They thought they would lose their power to the Inquisition.

In 1559 Pope Paul IV issued a list of books which the Roman Catholic Church thought were written by heretics. This was called the *Index*. A longer list of books was published by Pope Pius IV in 1564. This list included three-quarters of all the books printed in Europe at the time. Mostly the *Index* was a failure. People still printed and bought books that had been banned.

Paul IV

Pope Paul IV (1476–1559) was born Gian Pietro Caraffa. He became a cardinal in 1536 and reorganized the Inquisition. He became Pope in 1555. He was a violent and hard man, believing in the continued power of the Pope. He hated the Habsburg family who ruled Spain and parts of Italy. By working with the French against Charles V he helped to split the great Catholic countries of Europe.

Paul IV was defeated by the Spanish in 1557, but his hatred continued. His refusal to compromise with any Protestants actually helped the victory of Protestants in England. He encouraged racist treatment of the Jews. He tried to reform parts of the Church but made so many enemies that the reforms had only limited effect.

Members of the Inquisition in procession in Spain and the burning of heretics. From a Spanish enquiry, 1560.

6.3 Mystics in Spain

Protestants were not the only people who wanted a closer relationship with God. Many Roman Catholics wanted this too.

In Spain, **Teresa of Ávila** (1515–82) believed that it was possible to have a direct, personal experience of God. This idea was not new. Teresa is sometimes called a **mystic**. Mystics believe that by living holy lives of prayer, people can feel and enjoy the presence of God.

Teresa was a member of the **Carmelite Order** of nuns. In the 1550s she was very ill. During this time she believed she saw God. This is called a **vision**. After this experience she tried to encourage the other nuns to live purer lives. She travelled far and wide in Spain. In 1562 she set up a new community of nuns at the town of **Ávila**. When she died in 1582, she had started seventeen new communities.

A

SOURCE

The difference between the Roman Catholic and Protestant Reformation was between gradual and sudden change.

From 'The European Reformation' by E. Cameron, 1991.

B

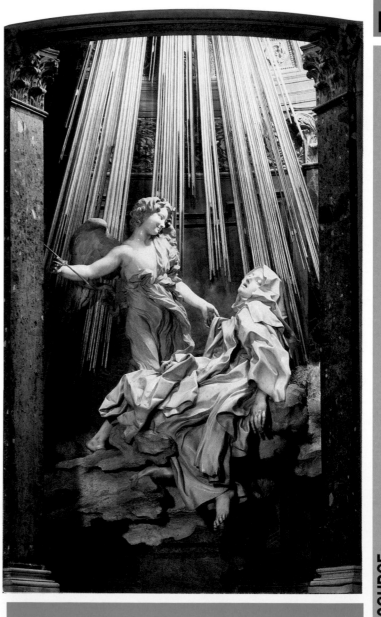

'Ecstasy of Saint Teresa' by Bernini (sculpted 1644–52). This statue was made to show Teresa experiencing a vision of God's love.

SOURCE

Some Roman Catholics distrusted Teresa. They felt that if a person had a direct relationship with God, they might not need the priests of the Church. Although Teresa was a Roman Catholic, she worried many powerful Church members. In 1561 the **Spanish Inquisition** seized a book she was writing about her beliefs. She only got it back with the help of the Spanish king.

Teresa wrote a number of books. One was called *The Way of Perfection*, published in 1565. *The Interior Castle* was published in 1567. In this book she said that a person's life is like a **castle**, and that God is like the **keeper of the castle**. By pure living and praying, a person could feel the power of God in their lives.

Protestants were not happy with Teresa's ideas. They felt they relied too much on a person's feelings and imagination. However, many people in Spain liked what she said. Her ideas promised people a closer relationship with God. Some of these people might have turned to Protestant ideas if it had not been for Teresa. Her beliefs encouraged them to stay in the Roman Catholic Church.

John of Yepes (1500–69) thought that Teresa's ideas were right. He is often remembered by the name **John of the Cross**. He was a preacher in a part of Spain called **Andalusia**. Like Teresa, John believed that a person could have a personal experience of the power of God. He made contact with mystics who were **Muslims**. He thought they might know something about God which he could learn from. Like Teresa, he was not popular with some of the powerful leaders of the Spanish Church. In 1577 he was imprisoned for one year.

During the 16th century, many Roman Catholics became more interested in miracles and experiences of God. Some historians think that the Reformation made many Roman Catholics want more out of their religion and their Church, even though they still stayed loyal to the Pope.

C

SOURCE

An angel appeared to me. He carried a spear tipped with fire. He plunged the spear into my heart. I was left on fire with a great love for God.

Teresa describes her vision in 1561.

D

SOURCE

- Bodies which did not rot.
- Bones which healed.
- Nuns who floated in the air.
- Hearts which caught fire.

Some of the miracles accepted in the 16th-century Roman Catholic Church.

Bernini

Gian Lorenzo Bernini (1598–1680) was born in Naples, in Italy. Bernini was a sculptor, architect and painter. In 1619 he was employed making statues for the powerful Italian Borghese family. In 1623 he began to work for Pope Urban VIII. He sculpted statues for St Peter's Church in Rome. He also worked on public fountains in Rome.

His statue of St Teresa was made for the Cornaro Chapel in the Church of St Maria della Vittoria, in Rome. Bernini's churches were built so that these great statues dominated people's minds when they entered the church. Each statue was meant to show an experience of the power of God. Bernini died in Rome.

6.4 The Jesuits

Some of the most dedicated opponents of 16th-century Protestant ideas were the **Jesuits**. They were members of a Roman Catholic organization whose full name was **The Society of Jesus**.

The person who set up this organization was called **Ignatius of Loyola** (1491–1556). He had been a soldier but was badly wounded in 1521. While he was recovering he felt called by God to serve Christ. He hung up his sword before the altar of the Virgin Mary at Montserrat. He spent a year praying about what he should do, at the monastery of Manresa. He wrote a book called *Spiritual Exercises.* In it he wrote about how a Roman Catholic should be obedient to God and the Pope.

At first, Ignatius planned to travel to the **Middle East** to preach about Jesus to the people who believed in **Islam**. He wanted to **convert** the Muslim world to the Roman Catholic faith. In the end this plan did not work out. Instead he formed a group of men who were willing to do whatever the Pope asked them to do. In 1540 Pope Paul III said that he agreed with this idea.

The Jesuits' speciality was total personal obedience to the Pope. They swore to own nothing and never to marry. In 1556 there were 1,500 Jesuits. By 1626 there were 15,544. Ignatius encouraged the Jesuits to preach to non-Christians. Soon, though, the Jesuits were working hard to oppose Protestant ideas. They set up schools to spread Roman Catholic ideas. They opposed Protestants in **France**, modern **Belgium**, **southern Germany** and **eastern Europe**. Some Spanish Jesuits even thought it was right to murder Protestant rulers. This kind of murder is called **assassination**. In 1584 a leading Dutch Protestant – William of Orange – was assassinated.

In 1549 the Jesuits set up a base in **Bavaria**, southern Germany. They were encouraged by **Albert**, the Roman Catholic Duke of Bavaria. He wanted to stop Bavaria becoming Protestant. The Jesuits succeeded in stopping some of the worst things that were going on in the Roman Catholic Church there. They also defended Roman Catholic beliefs. Bavaria was prevented from becoming Protestant.

A SOURCE

I will believe that the white object I see is black if that is what I am told by the Church.

A comment made by Ignatius of Loyola in the 16th century.

B SOURCE

Give me a child until he is aged 7 and he will stay a Roman Catholic all of his life.

Jesuit saying from the 16th century.

C SOURCE

Obey the Pope and the Jesuit commander as unquestioningly as a dead person.

Jesuit saying from the 16th century.

D SOURCE

Teach us good Lord to serve you as you deserve. To give and not to count the cost. To fight and not to care about wounds. To toil and not to ask for rest. To work and not to ask for any payment except knowing that we do what you want, through Jesus Christ our Lord.

Prayer of Ignatius of Loyola, 1535.

Other Jesuits went abroad to preach to non-Christians. By the early 17th century, there were Jesuits all over the world, from **Japan** to **North** and **South America**.

The Pope sent other Jesuits to countries in Europe. Their job was to persuade the rulers to stay friendly with Rome. The Roman Catholic rulers of **France**, **Poland** and **Bavaria** had personal advisors who were Jesuits. These representatives of the Pope were called **legates**. Many Protestants hated and feared the Jesuits.

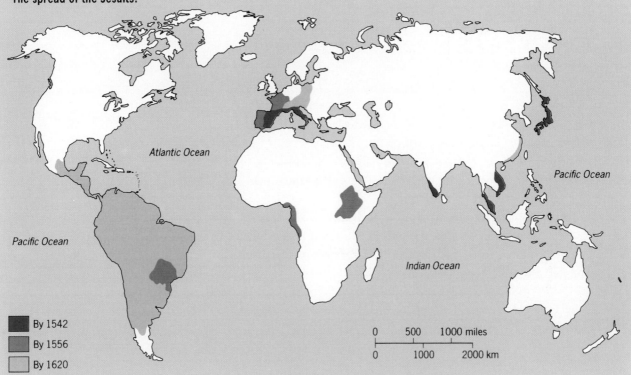

The spread of the Jesuits.

Atlantic Ocean

Pacific Ocean

Pacific Ocean

Indian Ocean

■ By 1542
■ By 1556
□ By 1620

0   500   1000 miles

0   1000   2000 km

William

William the Silent (1533–84) was born in Dillenburg, in the Netherlands. William was Prince of Orange and Count of Nassau. He opposed the attempts by the Spanish King Philip II to force the Dutch people to remain Catholics. In 1568 he lead the revolt of the Dutch Protestants against the Spanish Catholic government which ruled the Netherlands.

Supported by Calvinists in Germany and France and by the **'Sea Beggars'** (Dutch sailors who attacked Spanish ships and ports), he eventually became ruler (**stadholder**) of the United Provinces of the Netherlands in 1572. He found it hard to control his more extreme Calvinist supporters; this lost him support from Catholics. He was assassinated in 1584.

6.5 Building for God

By the end of the 16th century, it was clear that the Roman Catholic Church would survive. The Counter Reformation had reorganized the Church. Roman Catholics were more confident and clear about their beliefs. They were no longer afraid that Protestants would gain control in Europe.

This confidence showed itself in magnificently decorated churches. In **Rome** the painters **Raphael** and **Michelangelo** worked on superb paintings for churches. Their work can still be seen in the **Vatican Palace** and in the church of **St Peter**. The painter **Titian** worked in **Venice**. After about 1550 this kind of decoration increased. The artists **della Porta** and **Maderna** carried on the work in Rome. The artist **Tintoretto** continued the work in Venice.

The new churches were designed to amaze visitors. They were decorated in gold and silver. These churches were designed to make people aware of the beauty of God. They also reminded visitors of the power and wealth of the Roman Catholic Church. This type of decoration came to be called **baroque**.

Baroque churches were built in **Italy** and **Spain**. They were later also built in Roman Catholic parts of Germany, such as **Bavaria**. In the baroque churches the decorations and paintings reminded people of Roman Catholic beliefs.

Michelangelo

Michelangelo di Lodovico Buonarroti Simoni (1475–1564) was born in Caprese, in Italy. He was a painter, sculptor, architect and poet. He was one of the greatest artists in history and had a tremendous impact on art in western Europe. His work began in 1488 when he was trained by the Italian painter, Ghirlandajo. He worked in Rome between 1496 and 1529, producing a huge number of works of art. One of the most famous was the painting of the roof of the Sistine Chapel in Rome, which took him four years to complete.

From 1529 to 1534 he was involved in politics and fell out with the rulers of the Catholic Church. He was pardoned by Pope Clement VII, and went on to paint a dramatic wall painting, or **fresco**, *The Last Judgement*, in the Sistine Chapel (finished in 1541). He also designed the dome of St Peter's Church in Rome. He died in Rome.

A **SOURCE**

A visitor to them [baroque churches] will often find the dead body of a saint exposed on or under the altar. Death seems to be at the centre. The rich and powerful Church, rather than Christ, is at the centre.

From 'The History of Christianity' by R. Linder, 1990.

B **SOURCE**

The experience of Roman Catholic countries shows that one could leave the Middle Ages by several routes, of which the Reformation was only one.

From 'The European Reformation' by E. Cameron, 1991.

C **SOURCE**

While Calvinists stripped their chapels to bare essentials, baroque churches, filled with art, proclaimed the power of the Church of Rome.

From an article in 'National Geographic' by M. Severy, 1983.

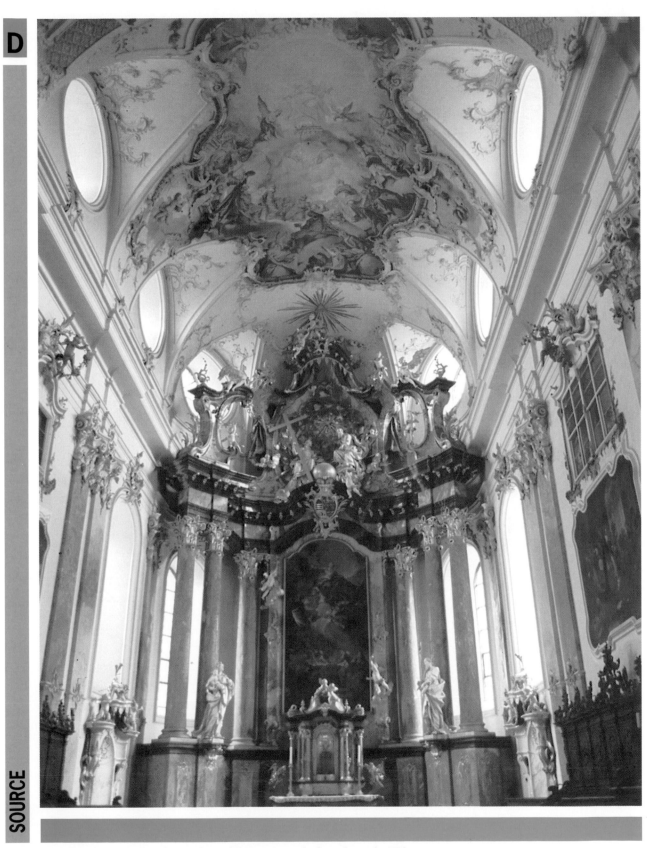

The inside of the baroque church at Odenwald, Germany, built in the early 17th century.

7.1 Reformation in the Netherlands

The modern countries of the Netherlands and Belgium, known then as the Low Countries, were ruled by the King of Spain in the 16th century. In the time of Charles V, the King of Spain was also the Holy Roman Emperor and a Roman Catholic.

In the Low Countries many people wanted to be free from Spanish control. Many of these people became Protestants. As early as 1523, Lutherans in the Low Countries were being killed because of their beliefs.

In 1555 Philip II, Charles V's son, became King of Spain. He used the Inquisition to attack those Protestants who opposed him. From 1566 communities of Protestants met openly, protected by armed guards. In 1565 a large group of noblemen met together to oppose the Spanish. They made an agreement called the **Compromise of Breda**. That year, revolts began against Spanish rule. Roman Catholic churches were attacked. Many Dutch merchants were also unhappy at having to pay large taxes to the Spanish.

In 1567 the **Duke of Alva** was sent to run the Low Countries for the Spanish king. The Duke killed many thousands of Protestants. On land, the Spanish soldiers – **tercios** – were hard to beat. At sea, though, the rebels were much stronger. They were helped by the English. The Spanish soldiers took terrible revenge on the towns which had opposed them. In 1576 the town of **Antwerp** was looted. This was known as **'The Spanish Fury'**. Soon even more areas of the Netherlands were in revolt. In the area of **Brabant** even Roman Catholics rose up against the Spanish.

The southern Netherlands were recaptured by the Spanish. The northern parts remained free. In 1581 the north declared that it was independent of Spain. This became the **Dutch Republic**. Its first leader was **William the Silent**. He was later murdered. Some English soldiers were sent to help the Dutch. The Spanish were now involved in a civil war in **France**. Also their planned invasion of England (the **Armada**) had failed in 1588. The Spanish were no longer strong enough to crush the Dutch. A new, mostly Protestant country had been born.

A SOURCE

A Dutch sailor's badge, 1574. It reads: 'Better Turkish than Papist' (Roman Catholic).

B SOURCE

The Prince of Orange has bewitched the minds of all men. They love him and fear him and wish to have him as their lord.

A letter from the Governor of the Netherlands to the Spanish king, in 1576. He is writing about William the Silent.

C SOURCE

The introduction of the Inquisition aroused the anger of a stubborn and proud people.

From 'Renaissance and Reformation' by V. Green, 1964.

Philip [of Spain] had a large army in the Netherlands. With this army he could control most of the country, except for the low-lying part criss-crossed with dykes. Here the rebels kept up a resistance. They often used English ports as a refuge.

From 'Past into Present' by M. Carter, C. Culpin and N. Kinloch, 1989.

Spanish soldiers kill Protestants in Haarlem, the Netherlands, 1567.

Philip II

Philip II (1527–98) was the son of the Emperor Charles V. He became King of Spain and the Spanish empire in 1555 while he was in the Netherlands, which was then ruled by Spain. He returned to Spain and ruled for the rest of his life from Madrid and his palace at El Escorial. He became King of Portugal in 1580.

Under his rule Spain supported the Counter Reformation and tried to defend the Catholic Church. It was his attempt to do this in the Netherlands which caused the revolt there. He also fought wars with the Muslim Ottoman Empire between 1571–8 and sent the Armada to try to invade England in 1588. Despite failures, such as the destruction of the Armada, Spain remained a powerful country at the time of his death in 1598.

7.2 Reformation in France

Protestant ideas spread to France. By 1540 there were a large number of Protestants in the country. One of their leaders was **Admiral Coligny**, an important French nobleman. These French Protestants were called **Huguenots**.

France became divided. Many nobles, merchants and some workers in the towns supported the new ideas. In the countryside, though, most peasants still supported the Roman Catholic Church. In 1561 the French government complained to the Calvinist Church in Geneva. This Church had been encouraging Protestants in France.

Some French noblemen supported the Protestants as a way of getting at the Roman Catholic King of France. They were called '**political Huguenots**'. From 1559 the reigning king was a child – Charles IX. This meant that the country did not have a strong government. The political Huguenots wanted power.

In 1562 a **civil war** broke out. In the town of **Toulouse**, 3,000 Huguenots were murdered by Roman Catholics. In other towns Huguenots wrecked Roman Catholic churches. The leader of the French Roman Catholics was the **Duke of Guise**. He was murdered in 1563. For almost 30 years France was torn apart by the civil war.

In 1589 Henry IV became king. He was a Protestant. The French Roman Catholics asked for help from Roman Catholic Spain. It looked as if the civil war would get worse. In 1593 Henry changed his religion and became a Roman Catholic. Most Huguenots were horrified. Henry said he did it for peace. He promised to reform the Roman Catholic Church. In 1598 Henry published the **Edict of Nantes**. In this he promised that both Roman Catholics and Protestants had the right to live peacefully in France.

The Huguenots had the right to have their own schools and law courts. They were even allowed to keep some fortresses to protect themselves. The Edict of Nantes was very important. It offered a chance for different religious groups to live together in the same country.

A SOURCE

But for the war, France would now be Huguenot, because the people were rapidly changing their faith. But when they [the Huguenots] passed from words to weapons and began to rob, destroy and kill, the people began to say: 'What kind of religion is this?'

An extract from a report by the Ambassador of Venice, 1569.

B SOURCE

It's worth going to a Roman Catholic mass to get control of Paris.

*Henry IV is reported to have said this in 1593. (A **mass** is a Roman Catholic service.)*

C SOURCE

I am entering the Church not to live in it but to clean it.

Henry IV speaking to worried Huguenots in 1593.

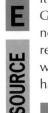
It is the lot of the Church of God to endure blows and not to strike them. But remember, it is an anvil which has worn out many hammers.

Theodore Beza, one of the leaders of the Church at Geneva and an advisor to French Huguenots, speaking in 1562.

Beza

Theodore Beza (1519–1605), born in France, was a leading Protestant writer and thinker. After studying law at Orleans he worked as a lawyer in Paris until 1548. Then he had a religious conversion after recovering from a serious illness.

Beza went to live in Geneva and joined Calvin, who was in the middle of the great changes that he carried out there. In 1559 he helped Calvin start the Geneva Academy to train Calvinist preachers and thinkers. He studied the Bible in Greek and his writings were used by the translators of the King James Bible in 1611. He was a strong minded man who continued Calvin's work.

SOURCE

The painting is by Jean Perrissin, 1565, and shows the inside of the Huguenot church at Lyons in southern France. It was called the Lyons Temple. The preacher wears a hat and his talk is timed using an hourglass.

7.3 The Massacre of St Bartholomew's Day

On the night of August 23 1572, over 3,000 **Huguenots** were murdered in Paris by Roman Catholics. This is known as the **Massacre of St Batholomew's Day**. Why did this massacre take place? How did people react to what happened?

Between 1562 and 1570 there was fighting in France between Protestants and Roman Catholics (see Unit 7.2). King Charles IX of France was only a child and his mother **Queen Catherine** worked hard to stop the king being controlled by either the extreme Protestants or the extreme Catholics.

In 1572 Queen Catherine was very worried. The Protestant leader **Coligny** had become popular with the king. Coligny wanted France to attack the Spanish in the Netherlands. The queen thought that this would be a disaster for France. Coligny also encouraged disagreements between King Charles and his brothers. This angered the queen who wished to get rid of Coligny.

B **SOURCE**

Those who organized the Massacre of St Bartholomew's Day acted in a panic. Instead of destroying the Huguenots, the massacre was the start of a fourth war.

From 'A History of Europe', by H. Fisher, 1935.

A late 16th-century Protestant picture of the massacre.

A **SOURCE**

C

SOURCE

An early 19th-century picture showing the murder of Coligny.

D

SOURCE

Catherine, fearful for her own safety between the two groups [Huguenots and extreme Catholics], decided on the awful step of trying to wipe out one of them.

From 'The Early Modern World', by C. Strong, 1968.

E

SOURCE

It is best seen as an act of desperation by a clever woman who had momentarily lost her head. But would she have hit on such a solution if it had not already been discussed by her friends?

From 'Europe Divided', by J. Elliott, 1968.

Queen Catherine was afraid that if the king became too friendly with the Huguenots he might be overthrown by the extreme Catholic nobles who hated the Protestants. The queen and her children were Catholics but feared these nobles.

The French Huguenots and some later historians have argued that Queen Catherine planned to kill the Protestant leaders long before it happened. She may have hoped that the extreme Protestants and extreme Catholics would destroy each other and leave her in peace.

Other historians have argued that in fact Catherine did not intend it to happen this way. They think that the whole situation got out of control. On August 22 the Huguenot leader Coligny was shot. There is evidence that the queen encouraged this. She was frightened by Coligny's influence over the king. However, Coligny was only wounded. Many Huguenots were in Paris at the time and were very angry about this. It may be that the queen panicked. She struck at them before they could act. Extreme Catholics were encouraged to kill leading Huguenots, including Coligny. This turned into a terrible massacre and spread to many French cities. Thousands of innocent Huguenots were murdered. Protestants everywhere were shocked. However, **Pope Gregory XIII** was delighted, as was the Catholic King of Spain.

Paré

Ambroise Paré (1510–90) was a French Protestant surgeon. He was saved from the massacre of the Huguenots because he was a skilful man who served the French king. It was Paré who first stopped treating gunshot wounds with boiling oil – and found that more of his patients survived. He also tied arteries after amputations rather than burning them with hot irons (**searing**). He used surgery only when absolutely necessary and introduced artificial limbs.

7.4 Europe Divided

The Reformation has often been blamed for dividing Europe. The Reformation split the Christian Church. The countries of Europe had to take sides. Before the Reformation, people felt that they were part of **Christendom**. After the Reformation, they thought of themselves as Protestants or Roman Catholics. Many Protestants could not agree among themselves. Calvinists disagreed with Lutherans. Both disagreed with the Anabaptists.

There was fighting between the Roman Catholics and Protestants in the 1540s and 1550s. It only ended when both sides admitted that Germany could not be united over religion again. In the 17th century, there were even more terrible wars.

The Counter Reformation tried to stop the spread of the new ideas. In some areas it was successful. **Bavaria**, **Poland**, **Austria**, **France**, **Belgium** and **Bohemia** were stopped from becoming Protestant. Many Protestants were killed or expelled. In countries such as Spain and Italy, the Roman Catholic Church became better organized than ever before.

It is wrong, though, to think that Europe was split only between Protestants and Roman Catholics. Many old quarrels and rivalries between nations carried on, as they had before the Reformation. The **Spanish** fought in every big European war between 1500 and 1659. They fought the Protestant Dutch for 80 years and the Roman Catholic French for 50 years. In the 16th century, the **French** were happy to help the German Protestants. They did this to make problems for their enemy, the King of Spain. At times, the King of France was an ally of the Protestants in Germany and the Turkish members of the Islamic religion.

Europe was divided between the north and the south. In the north, several countries became Protestant. In the south, they stayed Roman Catholic. In the north, countries such as England and the Dutch Republic began to develop **Atlantic** trade and to expand their **economies**. The economies of Spain and Italy had stopped growing. These differences were beginning to happen before the Reformation. Some historians think that the Reformation added to a split that was happening anyway.

This was a split between **middle class** merchants and craftspeople and **peasant** farmers who lived on land owned by rich people called **aristocrats**.

SOURCE A

The Protestant problem usually had to take a back burner to crises in Italy, or Spain, or to the Turkish threat.

Professor H. Rabe, 1983, talking about why the Emperor Charles V did not crush the Protestants.

SOURCE B

At the heart of Muslim and Christian weakness was their own political disunity.

From 'The Struggle for World Power' by W. Woodruff, 1981.

SOURCE C

The leaders of the Protestant Reformation usually came from the middle classes but those of the Roman Catholic Reformation were aristocrats.

From 'Christianity Through the Centuries' by E. Cairns, 1981.

Europe in 1610, showing the religious divisions nearly 100 years after the Reformation started.

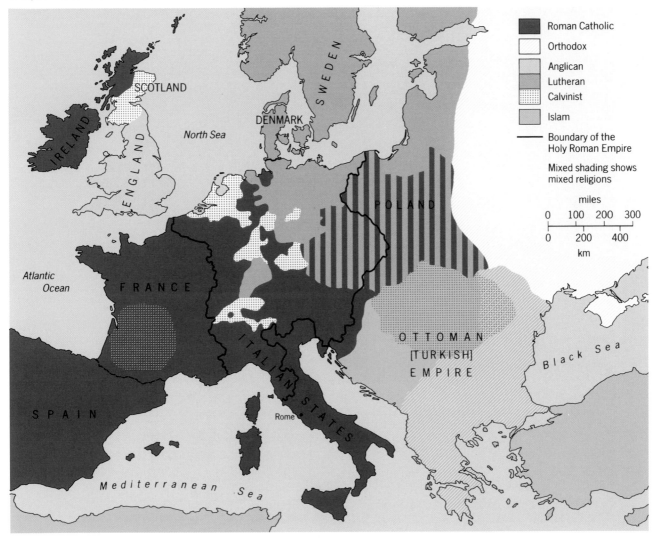

Legend:
- Roman Catholic
- Orthodox
- Anglican
- Lutheran
- Calvinist
- Islam
- —— Boundary of the Holy Roman Empire
- Mixed shading shows mixed religions

miles: 0 100 200 300
km: 0 200 400

SCOTLAND, SWEDEN, DENMARK, North Sea, IRELAND, ENGLAND, POLAND, Atlantic Ocean, FRANCE, ITALIAN STATES, OTTOMAN [TURKISH] EMPIRE, Black Sea, SPAIN, Rome, Mediterranean Sea

Don John

D

SOURCE

In 1571 the Turks captured the island of Cyprus from the Venetians. This led to the formation of a Christian league which annihilated the Turkish fleet in the great battle of Lepanto.

From 'Pursuit of Power' by J. Davis, 1970.

Don John of Austria (1547–78) was born in Regensburg, in modern Germany. He was the illegitimate son of Emperor Charles V and a merchant's daughter. After his birth he was taken from his mother and brought up in secrecy in Spain. When Charles died, his heir, Philip II, gave John land and wealth, and publicly treated him as a brother. Don John was handsome and popular. In 1569 he was made commander of the Spanish armies fighting in Granada, a part of Spain. In 1571 he was made commander of the ships belonging to Spain, Venice and the Pope, and fought Muslims in the Mediterranean. Later that year he defeated a Muslim fleet at the battle of Lepanto. He also fought in the Netherlands.

7.5 The Impact of the Reformation

A

SOURCE

Jesus as painted by the Dutch painter Rembrandt, 1606–69. It shows Jesus looking like a real Jewish man. Before this, most painters had made him look like a European with a halo.

The ideas of the Reformation changed history. The Roman Catholic Church was no longer the one Church in Europe. People who became Protestants believed they would only get to heaven if they sincerely believed in God. They did not need to rely on a priest or the Pope. This made what individuals thought and did much more important.

Many rulers were glad to become free of the power of the Pope. Some German rulers used Protestant ideas as an excuse for rebelling against the Roman Catholic Holy Roman Empire. People began to read the Bible and worship God in their own language. Soon, more and more books were being written in modern languages. In Germany the language of the new Bible helped people to decide on what was 'proper' German. There was also better education.

B O God, if Luther is dead who will explain to us the Gospel [the Good News about Jesus].

SOURCE

A comment made by the German artist Albrecht Dürer, 1521.

C You should read Luther to know whether he is right or wrong. We read everything.

SOURCE

Roman Catholic monk at the German monastery of Munnerstadt, 1983.

The Roman Catholic Church changed, too. The **Counter Reformation** made the Church better organized and more confident. Roman Catholics, like the **Jesuits**, carried Roman Catholic beliefs to thousands of people in **Asia**, **Africa** and **South America**. Many of these countries are still Roman Catholic today.

In many Protestant countries, ideas about art changed. Paintings and drawings became much more lifelike. They carried the message that God was interested in every aspect of life and the world. Artists like **Dürer** in the 16th century and **Rembrandt** in the 17th century were influenced by Protestant ideas.

Some historians feel that because Luther opposed the revolutionary Protestants he helped to make the ruling princes stronger than ever. In Germany the Lutheran Church did what it was told by the rulers. The beliefs of poorer people, like the Anabaptists, were crushed. This happened in many Protestant countries. The ideas of the Reformation often had least support among the **peasants**.

Some of the effects of the Reformation.

The Pope lost authority over many rulers.

The Church was split.

The rulers were more powerful.

For many people, what was most important was what an individual believed.

Many Protestants disagreed with each other. They would not listen to each other's ideas.

Dürer

Albrecht Dürer (1471–1528) was born in Nürnberg, in modern Germany. Dürer was a famous painter and printmaker. He lived for most of his life in Nürnberg but also visited Italy twice.

Dürer was responsible for creating the decorated panels of altars and other religious pictures. His pictures were brilliantly put together, realistic and eye-catching. He produced portraits too, the most famous of which was his self-portrait, made in 1498.

Dürer also made prints of his pictures by engraving them on copper and wood. One of his copper prints – made in 1513 – can be seen in Unit 2.4 of this book.